In the Jumble

The joys of finding, buying and wearing

second hand clothes.

Victoria Lochhead

Copyright © 2016 Victoria Lochhead

All rights reserved.

ISBN:1539629570

ISBN-13: 978-1539629573

DEDICATION

For my own personal superstars - Andrew and the real Frankie & Ruby – thank you cherubs x

also

For Mrs Wiseman - because I promised.

I can tell you now that I wouldn't have got half as far as putting one word on the page if it had not been for the support and encouragement from my friends at BBB Success Groups, and it certainly would not have been this much fun! Thank you George. Tracey, and fellow Success Group members.

CONTENTS

	Introduction	6
1	How I found the jumble	9
2	Making choices – what we buy, how much we buy and where we buy from	21
3	Deciding to go second hand – advantages and pitfalls of second hand shopping	31
4	Your game plan - how to create a useful second hand wardrobe	39
5	Getting out there – how to shop second hand and get the most out of it	55
6	Caring for and adapting your treasures	73
7	What you can expect to happen after a year	91

"I'm really interested in fashion but at the same time I find it quite competitive. Second-hand stuff leaves you more open to whatever your own personal style is rather than feeling dictated to by shops." Sophie Ellis-Bextor

"Buy less. Choose well. Make it last. Quality, not quantity. Everybody's buying far too many clothes." —Vivienne Westwood

"I'm a get-a-dress-at-the-thrift-shop-but-open-a-bottle-of-champagne kind of person." Helen Mirren

INTRODUCTION

When I was thinking of writing an introduction to this book, I didn't want to begin with a formal introduction and some boring CV. So, I thought I'd start by telling you some interesting stuff, and you can work the rest out from there.

My favourite colour is green, but I don't have green fingers (my sister got those in the genetic shake-down). When I was very small I had a teddy that played 'Hey Jude' from a wind up mechanism in it's back, and it's been lost for about 35 years. I've just taught myself to make Pavlova (thanks to Mary Berry) and I have a current fondness for chocolate covered rice cakes. I think that will do for now, the rest you'll pick up as we go along, I'm sure. I suppose I'd better let you know that I'm also a trained personal stylist, not just some random rice-cake loving, bear hunting, pavlova making woman in green who's written a book about second hand clothes and how to wear them.

That would just be weird.

I like writing. In fact I should have added that to my interesting list. I write a lot, but I particularly wanted to write something about my passion for treasure hunting in second hand shops for beautiful things to wear. I wanted to share my stories and the things I've learned along the way, so that others could either give it a go themselves if they've never done it before, or laugh along with me at my blunders if they have. I also wrote this book because as a personal stylist, I do have a few tricks up my sleeve about how to develop your own style. This is so relevant when you're doing any kind of shopping, but especially so in the cut price world of second hand style, that I wanted to share a few hints and tips with you so that you get the most out of your new and beautiful recycled wardrobe.

I believe that looking amazing need not cost the earth, in both financial and environmental senses of the word. If you understand your own unique rules of colour, shape and style, then it is perfectly possible to shop anywhere. And if you can shop anywhere then the ultimate in guilt free shopping awaits any intrepid explorer in the form of charity shops and their rather more physically demanding cousin, the jumble sale.

This book will show you how to shop second hand, what to look for that's right for you and your style, where to go, and how to strike gold and find treasure. It will give you tips on how to look after your finds, and how to bring it all together in a wardrobe that works for you.

If you've never even considered shopping second hand before, this book is a perfect first step on that delightful journey. Old hands at second hand might enjoy the styling and clothes care tips, and anyone who is thinking that the way we buy clothes right now cannot possibly be sustainable might enjoy a dip between these pages. For our American friends across the water, the problem of too many textiles ending up in landfill is just as great (the average American discards an average of 70lbs of unwanted clothes & textiles every year according to www.weardonaterecycle.org). All of the tips in the book may well be useful to anyone who'd like to recycle more, whether at a jumble sale or a thrift store. In fact, if you're reading this outside of the UK, wherever you see the words 'charity shop' or 'second hand shop' please mentally replace it with your own brand of second hand cool, and please excuse my Earl Grey sipping Englishness, because all of the information nuggets in this book apply, wherever you are shopping in the world.

I've written it from my own female perspective, but chaps, you can apply exactly the same principles of wardrobe management and colour to your own styling in order to get out there and enjoy the delights of second hand shopping. In fact more guys in the gang would be great, there's never anyone rummaging through the jumble on the men's table – you'll have the place to yourselves (until the word gets out).

If you've got a teenage son or daughter who thinks that something new is a weekly necessity and is achieved by nipping down to H&M and spending a fiver, who perhaps hasn't yet considered where those clothes have come from, what it has taken to make it, and what happens to it when they've got bored with it, then please buy them a copy of this book to read. The more of us who are aware of the true cost of clothes production, the better, and the younger amongst us seem to be really good at spreading the word online. Let's start a movement together, a revolution, a change.

One t-shirt at a time.

CHAPTER 1: HOW I FOUND THE JUMBLE

In 2006 I found myself staring into my wardrobe on the verge of tears. At my feet were just about every pair of trousers I owned, and not one of them fitted me any more.

I'd had my second daughter about six months earlier, and I was due to return to work the following week. My shape and size had changed so the only things I could still get into were a pair of maternity jeans and a pair of pyjamas. I didn't think my colleagues would be too impressed with me rolling back to work in a pair of tartan PJ's so I reluctantly decided I would have to get something new. The idea of trundling along to the shops in my baby sick t-shirt to find something to fit me was far from appealing. Like booking a wax, or opening the latest credit card bill.

So I did what I always did when I got a bit stuck because I needed some clothes but didn't know what I was looking for and didn't have much spare cash; I went to the Next sale. I managed to get a suit and a couple of tops so I thankfully wouldn't need the PJ's, but the pale grey pinstripe suit did absolutely nothing for my confidence, my colouring, or my figure.

A good friend of mine tactfully suggested a trip to see an image consultant to sort me out. That visit completely transformed the rather dim view I'd fallen into that shopping for clothes was tantamount to torture and completely unnecessary because clothes didn't really matter. Actually the clothes themselves don't, but how they make you feel and what they do for your confidence absolutely does – I know that now! That day I learned why everyone always thought I was ill when I wore black, and how I've always looked a bit startled when I try pink lipstick. I realized I should never have dyed my hair that shade of blonde, and I discovered that my love of flares was completely natural, in fact encouraged, as was a hankering for wooden jewelry and chunky knit jumpers.

Looking back now, I can see that learning my rules of what suited me and complimented the natural me was something of a mild epiphany. It really helped me to define and express who I felt I was at the time, to merge all the roles I had (wife, mum, sister, employee, friend, daughter etc.) and to feel more of a whole person. I changed my hair, wiped off the baby vomit, bought some new clothes and ditched the utility trousers – why was I even wearing those? I looked like one of those outdoor-y adventure mothers who would light fires and carry their babies in various impressive body slings. That wasn't me at all; I guess I just thought all the pockets would be useful.

After my turnaround I remember buying a new outfit from Jigsaw for my baby's christening. It was a pair of linen trousers and a metallic loose knit top, which I put a teal belt over. It was the first time in a very long time that I felt great about how I looked. I really started to think 'hell, yeah, this is me people!' It was a fantastic feeling that I had completely lost in my life, and I know now that it was an important feeling. Wearing clothes that really express who we are is what makes us stand tall, chin up. It's a caffeine hit of confidence right between the eyes. It's you, going out into the world wearing your identity. When that happens the world says, "OK then, well this is someone awesome." The way other people interact and respond to you changes, improves, and this feedback makes you feel even more confident in your new skin.

It's quite amazing actually.

I have of course made mistakes along the way, plenty. That day I went to work in a bright floral silk dress with a grass green cardigan and magenta shoes was definitely a mistake. Hawaiian Show Girl looks are no longer in my repertoire after that disastrous management meeting. But looking back, the mistakes have been as useful as the triumphs (dark brown wool crepe dress that made me look ever so slightly curvy and got lots of compliments springs instantly to mind) because that's how we learn. And I can promise you that I've learned a lot.

My image consultant experience gave me a huge boost of confidence when I needed it most, re-ignited my love and enjoyment of being creative with clothes, and then some time later even led me to seek out the amazing Gail Morgan in order to train as an image consultant myself. Lucky me, I now get to help other people re-love their clothes (and themselves) every day.

The main thing my experience with an image consultant taught me, and what I now try to teach my clients is actually not really about clothes at all. It made me think more about who I was, and what messages I wanted to get across about myself. It made me more aligned with my true self, and able to express that through what I wear. I stopped having a wardrobe of clothes that were earmarked for 'work', 'home', 'best', and 'going out' and just started having clothes that were earmarked for me, that I could wear across different roles I had in my life. I felt happier and more confident, and freely able to express that through my wardrobe. Yes, I was a different shape, and yes I was a couple of sizes bigger than I had been pre-baby, and yes at the bottom of my handbag was a couple of broken crayons and a half eaten biscuit, but suddenly that was OK. I realized I had been using my change in size as an excuse to avoid shopping, mirrors, clothes, getting dressed. Partly because I was, well, exhausted, but partly because it meant facing up to thinking about myself and who I was, and who I would become when I went back to work. Underneath all of that avoidance was a fear that I wouldn't be able to handle being a working mum. Also probably some dread. I loved my job, but there's a whole heap of guilt thrown in when you have to drop your beautiful blonde babies off at a nursery in order to do the work. And I was also really enjoying my maternity leave – if I had been really honest with myself, I probably didn't want to go back to work at all, and was avoiding making any decisions or provisions for it. Wow, all those thoughts just milling around under the surface of me not wanting to find something nice to wear to work.

This leads me to an interesting discovery I've made.

Clothes are never the issue.

When a client comes to see me with a wardrobe dilemma, I know that it's never actually about the clothes. Unless they turn up naked, I'm assuming they do have garments they can put on most days to preserve their modesty. It's not a lack of clothes that's the problem. It's a lack of clothes that reflect who they are now, or who they want to be. Under every clothes dilemma is a person dilemma. After all, our clothes are our outer surface, and our outer surface (whether we realize it or not) reflects what's going on inside.

Often with clients that come to me, something has changed in their lives. Maybe they've got a new job, a new partner, or had a baby, or the kids have left home. This change has challenged them, led them to question their identity, who they are, what their role is and how they fit into the new scheme of things. Their clothes simply haven't caught up with them yet, and they need some new ideas of what to wear to fit with their image of this new person emerging from their cocoon.

What I've learned is that at the root of most 'what to wear' dilemmas is actually more of a 'who do I want to be' question. Answer that, and the clothes dilemmas go away.

When I'd got my head around who I was as a working mum, and what that meant in terms of what I wore, I actually began to enjoy shopping again. But working mothers have large nursery bills to pay and not much spare cash, and I wasn't enjoying shopping in the places I could actually afford to shop in. I'm the kind of person who shops with their hands – I like to feel the fabric, touch it, decide if it will be soft and comfortable, or if it will generate a Mohican from all the static it creates.

I'm sure this fear of man-made fabrics stems from when I was a child. As a child of the 70's nearly everything in my life was that highly flammable polyester type material, and one night I went to bed in my polyester nightdress with polyester sheets on the bed.

I thought there was lightening in the bed, I could actually see the static electricity bouncing between the sheets and my nightdress. My mother thought I'd made it up when I shouted that I was on fire and sent me straight back to bed.

No more lightening bolts for me, thank you very much.

I wanted nice fabrics, I wanted clothes that were a good fit, and I wanted things that would last, but I simply couldn't afford them.

One day, as I was trundling along with my pushchair to meet some mum friends for a coffee, my eye was drawn to the clothes displayed in the window of the Cancer Research shop. Before I knew it, I'd wheeled my pushchair in and started browsing around. I found a lovely Monsoon green wrap top and a set of green, orange and wood beads and I spent a total of £5.49. Light bulbs were going off in my head. If I wanted to find clothes that I could enjoy wearing and spend hardly any money, why hadn't I thought of it before? I could shop second hand! The idea wasn't new to me, I'd practically grown up on charity shop finds and hand me downs. But in that moment, I wondered if I could do it again as an adult?

When I was a child we didn't have much money and it was a treat to go to a jumble sale with 20p tucked in my hand. My Nan would take us most Saturdays and we'd come home with real treasures; a jigsaw puzzle (often with pieces missing, which we seemed to enjoy as a sort of puzzle roulette), or some baby clothes for a doll. But my Nan would spot a jumper she could unravel and use the wool for something else (probably a multi-coloured cardigan for which she was quite famous), or at the very least to keep us quiet for an hour making pom-poms. Or she'd find (joy of joys) some fabric we could cut up and make into book covers or picnic blankets for our teddy bear picnics.

Through my rose tinted spectacles, jumble sales (and roller skates) were highlights of my childhood.

Now and again, we'd find a dress, or more often, an older cousin would have a clothes clear out, and we'd be presented with a big black bag of hand-me-downs that we were allowed to choose whatever we wanted from. This was like Christmas to my younger sister and I; and she had a double whammy because she knew that whatever I chose would eventually trickle down to her anyway.

One year I found a brown and gold striped dress, which had a delightfully 80's swag detail across the neck, which I thought was to die for. I wore it and wore it and wore it, and then my sister wore it, and then we passed it on to someone else. I'll say one thing for those early man-made fabrics – they might set your hair on fire, but they certainly were completely indestructible.

In the small town I grew up in, our high street was limited. We had plenty of hairdressers, newsagents and estate agents shops, but there was one clothes shop in our town (where I worked on Saturdays dressing the windows, but I could never afford the clothes that were sold), and everything else was a charity shop. If I wanted to spend my money on something more than magazines and sweets, the only places I could look round was the charity shops. Many a Saturday afternoon saw my sister, my cousin and I diving in and out of charity shops, looking for interesting things.

As I grew up and started to save for university, a lack of money led me to start searching in charity shops for things I could adapt to fit the current trends. My mum had given me an old Singer sewing machine and I remember cutting out pictures of outfits from the Littlewoods catalogue. I'd then try to find similar things in charity shops I could alter to look like the pictures. A blue spotted dress that I turned into a shorts suit was a particular hit (although it did take me about half an hour to get out of it every time I needed the loo). I loved adapting clothes that someone else didn't want anymore and making them into something new that I could enjoy wearing. It was creative, fun, and cheap – and not many activities fall into all three of those categories.

When I left university and got a job, I had more money and no time. This is not a good mix for fuelling a charity shop habit. I needed clothes for work fast and I could afford to pop in to M&S and buy something. So I did. I got out of the charity shop habit and into the high street. And for a while that was OK. The only time I went near a charity shop was to donate my unwanted clothes. But when I think back now, that transition to shopping on the high street signaled the start of the slide. The creativity moved out of my wardrobe and went to live with someone who had time for it. My clothes became useful, practical, functional. Who wants a wardrobe based on those adjectives? Yes, I looked smart at work every day, but so did everyone else. That's what had happened. In an effort to conform in my job, I had such a conformist wardrobe, that I had completely lost sight of the clothes I liked, and I think that over time that led me to lose sight of who I was too.

After my experience with an image consultant, with my combined newfound confidence and my lack of cash came a rekindling of my love of finding beautiful things from charity shops. I realized quickly that it is perfectly possible to dress amazingly well from other people's unwanted items, and I began to look forward to going out to hunt for something second hand, enjoying the thrill of the chase and the joy of finding a treasure. I gradually shopped less and less in Fat Face and more and more in charity shops. My confidence grew further, and by the time my girls were older, and I'd left my job to start my image consultancy business, I was a fully-fledged second hand junkie.

I started my image consultancy business Frankie & Ruby firstly because I had finally admitted to myself that I wanted a career I could fit round my babies rather than the other way around. Secondly I started it because I wanted to help other women. I wanted to help them to make sense of the endless choices of what to wear. I wanted to give them that skipping down the street feeling, that easy morning of picking out something to wear rather than heaping everything on the bed and reaching for the Sauvignon.

Initially, I was reluctant about sharing my love of second hand shopping with my clients, I mean, who had ever heard of a stylist who buys things from charity shops? Surely my clients would be expecting me to take them shopping in boutiques and on designer rails and persuading them to part with a months salary to look good?

This little idea was burning away inside me, because I knew that looking fabulous needn't cost the earth. People were noticing and commenting on what I was wearing, and the truth came out – I started sharing my treasures, and my love of dressing from charity shops.

What I've realized is that through my business, I can show my clients their unique rules of dressing, and then show them how to achieve that second hand. My clients love it. They love it that I can find them a whole new wardrobe for under £100, and some are happy to part with their hard earned cash to pay me to find treasures for them. Those that aren't into second hand, that's fine. I can take them to the high street and apply the same principles; I don't force anyone along to a Jumble sale if it's not their thing. But instead of it destroying my business as a stylist, sharing my love of second hand has brought me a unique, fun, interesting, and creative way of living and working that has the added benefit of helping a few lovely people along the way.

Today my wardrobe is probably around 80% sourced second hand and the rest is either stuff I've had for ages, or a few basic essentials I've bought new. When I get dressed in the mornings I feel confident in my choices and I have more than one possible outfit to wear. There's not a drop of baby sick, and I never have to resort to the tartan PJ's. I feel creative when I go shopping now, and not in a bonkers eccentric way, but most importantly, my wardrobe reflects me and who I am right now. I know I need new things to keep up with changes in me, but I also know they only have to be new to me. I don't have a huge wardrobe. At all. But I do have 2 sets of clothes, one Spring/ Summer and one Autumn/ Winter. I sort them twice a year and switch my wardrobe, carefully packing away the season we've just been through for 6 months. I find this an excellent way to stop getting bored of my clothes – I don't see them for six months of the year and absence does make the heart grow fonder, so they say. When my summer wardrobe comes out to play again at the start of spring, it's like having a giant shopping spree; everything feels new and exciting again. There's more on this in later chapters, but I find that from rekindling my love of second hand shopping, I've got a wardrobe that works, clothes that I love, a style that I think is ideal for me, and cash in my pocket. Result.

VICTORIA LOCHHEAD

CHAPTER 2: MAKING CHOICES

What we buy, how much we buy and where we buy from.

Lets start by making something very clear.

I am not an eco-warrior.

I don't live in a house made of old car tyres, nor do I go foraging for berries for dinner. I've never skip-dived, nor have I got a shower powered by rainwater. I'm a regular, run of the mill consumer. I'd like to be greener, I would. I recycle all my paper & glass, and I own a compost bin. I use bags for life, and I switch off my TV at the wall when it's not being used (much to the irritation of my family, who keep thinking the TV's broken.) I don't like the amount of packaging supermarkets use, and I'm sure I've invented an idea that cars should have solar panels on the roof. I do my bit, like everyone else, and, like everyone else I know that we could and should do a lot more to recycle. So, where better a place to start than with our clothes.

I can tell you for a fact that most of us just have too many.

I'm not easily moved to passionate speeches, but I do feel a mild rant coming on. If you're reading this book because you just want to know more about how to make your wardrobe more fun, useful organized and exciting, please move on. Start at chapter 3 and ignore this little high horse section I seem to feel compelled to include. If you're OK with it, read on, because I just want to set out the landscape for you about why I think buying second hand is such a no brainer hands down brilliant idea.

In my job as a personal stylist, I'm paid to go to peoples homes and help them sort out the muddle that too many clothes has caused in their lives. I've uncovered drawers, wardrobes, bags under the bed, boxes in the loft, suitcases just full of holiday clothes, more in the garage. Mountains and mountains of clothes. Now, even if you're really in to layering, I'm sure the average person in the northern hemisphere can only wear a maximum of 8 items of clothing at any one time. In fact, most of us only wear a paltry 20% of the clothes we own. The rest is hanging there, or squashed in a bag, gathering dust. And if it's a forgotten piece of fabric that's left to gather dust, it's nothing more than rags. That's how we treat the clothes we don't wear. What good are they to us, other than to serve as reminders of the time we foolishly spend a weeks wages in a little boutique in Brighton, or the time we could actually fit into those jeans? They leave us feeling a little guilty, and they take up valuable space in our lives and our thoughts. According to the brilliantly inspiring website www.loveyourclothes.org.uk in the average UK household nearly 1/3 of all clothing has not been worn in over a year. That's about £1,000 in cash sitting doing absolutely nothing except take up space.

Why is it that we seem to have too many clothes? Why is it that 1/3 don't get worn? In my experience, I would say that most of my clients wear around 20% of their wardrobe 80% of the time. Think about your wardrobe, do you have some favourites in there that you miss when they're in the wash? Do you have things hanging up that barely see the light of day?

In many countries, shopping for clothes for many people is a hobby (and a fun one too). Clothes shops are bright and attractive, music's playing, the clothes are beautifully displayed. It's very easy to while away a Saturday afternoon trying on and buying clothes. And now, clothes have got a lot cheaper, so this past time is available to more people more often. According to the website www.scratchhard.com the average price of clothes has decreased by 8.5% since 1992, and that's even when adjusted for inflation. Why wouldn't you go out and buy clothes when it's fun, exciting, and (now) relatively inexpensive?

When I was younger, clothes were quite expensive. I remember my mum allowing us to choose one dress each a year (yes, that's right – one new dress a year!) from the Littlewoods catalogue, which she would then pay off in weekly installments. We coveted those dresses, we wore them and wore them, and then passed them on to another cousin to wear and wear them. My mother had to work hard to pay off that bill (which would have had interest added on the weekly payments) because there was no way she could have afforded to take us to the shops and buy two dresses upfront.

These days, some high street new clothes don't seem to cost much more than a cappuccino. And if something doesn't cost much, how is it treated? Well, if it falls apart, does it really matter? It can just be thrown away. This seems to be happening a lot – in fact over the course of a year, the UK sends enough clothes to landfill to fill Wembley Stadium (www.bagtoschool.com). To landfill, that's not even recycling it into dusters or 70's style rag rugs or anything. Just chucked straight in the bin. So, do we hold these cheap clothes in high esteem? No, I don't think we do.

I'm not an ethical, environmentally conscientious clothes purchaser. Or, I wasn't. I used to shop in Primark, and Tesco's, Matalan and Peacocks. Places I could buy cheap clothes worked for me at times when I had no disposable income but needed to not be seen naked. I found though that shopping in this way brought me no lasting joy. I enjoyed wearing the clothes the first few times, but after that, I stopped caring about them. I think something happens in our brains when we think something is cheap and freely available – we stop caring about it. It doesn't matter, because replacements are inexpensive and easy to come by. I clearly remember thinking "well, if it falls apart, it doesn't matter because it's cheap." My expectation was that it would fall apart, almost that the clothes were disposable, temporary. I've even heard of people who shop their entire holiday wardrobe in Primark, totally prepared to dump the whole lot in the bin before the flight home. That is surely a disposable commodity, isn't it?

I don't feel that way about my secondhand treasures. They cost roughly the same as the Primark bargains, but I think because I know I won't find another one the same, and perhaps because they are hard searched for treasures, I value them more. For the same price as my cheap Primark dress that I'm expecting to fall apart, I can buy a second hand designer one and I will cherish it and the quality of its production.

I happen to really love fashion. I love seeing the creative edge of the clothing industry, what new ideas designers have come up with, and how those ideas trickle down onto the high street. But I'm not a slave to fashion. If something is really current, but doesn't suit my straight up and down body shape, I'll not touch it with a barge pole. If this season's must wear colour is grey, too bad. I'll not be seen in it. I love looking at fashion, but I don't have to or want to wear it. But I know that some people adore fashion, they love wearing the latest styles, they simply have to have this seasons range hanging in their wardrobes. Which is fine. If you love and cherish your clothes and like buying and wearing for each season, go ye ahead. But if you want to have ALL the fashion hanging in your wardrobe each season, hang on. Stop a minute. All the fashion? Really?

The fashion industry is not a charity, it's a business. We have two new season collections launched each year to keep clothes and styling new and fresh and exciting. Why? So that we go to the shops and we buy it! Fashion is there to encourage us to buy more new clothes each year, and inadvertently we then stop wearing what we were enjoying last year or last season, because it's not current. That chevron skirt you wore all last summer suddenly becomes redundant this year because it's no longer in fashion. It creates an inevitable churn in the clothing industry, which is completely necessary for new clothes sales, and unwittingly fuels the cast off end of the industry.

If, as a nation, we are managing to fill Wembley stadium every year with clothes and textiles that we just chuck in the bin, how much more are we discarding or not wearing? How much is given to charity shops, stuck into those recycling bags that come through the door every week, put in a textile bank, rummaged through at a jumble sale? How much is just sitting in our homes gathering dust?

Millions upon millions of pounds.

And when you think of the energy it takes to make each item of clothing (800 litres of water just to make one t-shirt!), then think of the energy it's taken to get those clothes to market in the first place, the production of the fabrics, dyeing, manufacture of the clothes, shipping, packaging, shop lighting, etc etc etc. All that energy, lying unloved and unused in the back of your wardrobe. It makes you want to go and get those clothes and give them a hug, doesn't it?

I recently saw a very interesting BBC2 program called "The Secret Life of your Clothes' which documented the journey our clothes took in their life cycle. The program highlighted how our clothes are made by some of the poorest people in the world, they come to the UK and are sold in our shops, worn and then donated to charity, and are sold abroad – to the poorest people in the world. Ghana alone receives almost £1million worth of our unwanted clothes every week, yes, you read that right, every week! While this second hand clothes mountain has fuelled a multi million pound industry all of it's own, the only reason it exists (I think) is because our clothes are too cheap in the first place and we are treating them more and more as disposable commodities.

My neighbour told me of a young lady who had lost a button from her jacket and so thrown the jacket in the bin. Apparently the girl didn't know how to sew on a new button, and as the jacket was only £4, she'd just popped out and bought an identical one. By this point in the conversation I am apoplectic on the floor. Not only was that a huge waste, but also the girl didn't know how to sew on a button? A button! And to add insult to injury, she's then gone out and bought an identical jacket. What if the button falls off this one? Is she just going to keep buying jackets until she gets one with secure buttons on?

I'd been thinking for a while that I didn't like the idea of Wembley stadium getting filled up with clothes every year, only to dig a hole and chuck them all in it. The button story tipped me over the edge. After a large G&T and a lie down in a dark room, I decided I would do something. Take some action, get involved. As far as I was aware we had several problems on the table:

1. We all have too many clothes

2. There are clothes in our wardrobe that are unloved, unworn, and gathering dust

3. It is possible now to buy new clothes very cheaply

4. Because of the low prices and easy availability of new clothes, it has become commonplace to view clothes as cheap and expendable, easily replaceable

5. It takes a whole lot of energy to make new clothes, and yet loads of clothes end up in the bin

6. If we want to stay in fashion, we simply must have the latest clothes in the shops, whether we need them or not, whether we have space for them or not, and whether they suit us or not.

7. Once we buy our new season clothes, we simply cannot wear last seasons clothes, so we get rid of them.

As a stylist and a re-discoverer of the joys of second hand clothes, my solutions are predictably simple:

1. Work out how to exist on less new clothes
2. Teach my clients the rules of their own unique style so they are only buying what suits them and not making expensive mistakes that gather dust in the wardrobe or blindly buying all the latest fashion.
3. Show others how to organize their wardrobes so that they can see what they have and utilize everything
4. Show clients how to make more outfits out of what they already have in their wardrobes
5. Encourage more people how to shop second hand, and how to buy new to them clothes from second hand sources.

I decided to test my solutions on myself. I didn't buy any new clothes (apart from the personal and the very basic) for a year, and instead I bought from eBay, second hand shops, charity shops and vintage shops. No one took me aside and told me I looked like a bag lady. I started a group on Facebook called Say No to New (rather rallying, don't you think?) to encourage others to join me, and this led to an interview with Good Housekeeping Magazine, and an interview with Anne Diamond on BBC Radio Berkshire. Get me.

Around the same time as I was coming up with slogans and designing placards, the Government launched its textile waste reduction initiative called Love Your Clothes. This brilliant organization is literally groaning with tips and ideas to make more of the clothes we already have, from recycling, to repurposing to (joy of joys) simple mending and laundering tips.

Music to my ears.

As a stylist, I am always poking around my clients wardrobes and helping them to de-clutter, get organized, and get rid of the things they don't want any more. I've been so amazed at how much is possible to clear out without making much of a dent in what people own, that after my year of Saying no to New I added a dress agency to my Frankie & Ruby business. When clients have a wardrobe clear out now, I sell on the clothes that are nearly new that they don't want any more. I love it, it's a bit like a dating agency, I take their unloved dress and find it a new partner who will love and cherish it.

I know that I'm not the only person who finds deep joy in a Jumble Sale poster, or a fizz of excitement at the prospect of a new charity shop. Others are out there, and more are coming on board every day. There are some fantastic ethical clothing projects out there that I wholeheartedly applaud:

Project 333 – (www.bemorewithless.com)

Project 333 is one such project, designed to help show people how it is completely possible to live with less clothing, by creating a capsule seasonal wardrobe from only 33 items of clothing.

Traid - (www.traid.org.uk)

Traid is a brilliant charity with second hand clothes shops positioned around London. Traid teams educate and inform on issues around textile recycling and they help fund projects to improve conditions and working practices in the textile industry around the world. On their website you can pledge what % of your wardrobe you commit to buy second hand, or you can take part in their second hand first week in November.

If by now you're thinking, "OK V, I hear you. I've read your story, and I've been equally appalled at the amount of textiles heading to a hole in the ground. I'm in and I'm going straight down to my Cancer Research shop to buy everything and start a fun and creative new second hand life." I'm just going to say hang on a minute. Just stop for a second. It's not all Cath Kidston prints and china teacups you know. I cannot send you out treasure hunting without being fully prepared. Otherwise you'll get inside the door, decide it's all too cluttered and walk straight back out, never to be seen again. No, we don't want that.

So, before you dash off to pick yourself up a few pieces of bargain vintage, please read on. I want to share some of the amazing benefits of second hand shopping with you, but also give you a heads up to some of the pitfalls.

CHAPTER 3: DECIDING TO GO SECOND HAND

Advantages and pitfalls of second hand shopping

So, just before you go dashing off to your local British Heart Foundation shop with your bag for life tucked under your arm, let's take a moment. Second hand shopping and styling is brilliant for lots of reasons. But there are also a few pitfalls I've discovered along the way that I'd like to share with you. I don't want you falling into any pits now.

So, first, here's the good stuff (incase you still need convincing).

RECYCLING

Not only does buying pre-loved clothes fill me with the kind of ecstatic bliss normally reserved for Ferrero Roche, but I happen to be particularly addicted to all the great other benefits that come from shopping in this way. Of course the first of these benefits has to be about recycling. I can walk into a charity shop and find a dress I love and then get an added thrill from knowing I'm helping reduce the number of clothes that end up in landfill, reducing the environmental burden of new clothes production, and therefore am literally saving the planet (heroic theme tune here). Well, maybe not quite saving the planet, but if lots of us changed our shopping habits, it's good to know that it can make a difference in the world and to planetary resources.

GIVING

It's also quite a nice feeling if I'm rummaging around a charity shop or jumble sale to know that the money I spend in the shop goes towards doing something good. Yes, yes, I can hear you, I know that a chunk of the money goes to running the shop, but ultimately, any profits from that endeavor can make a difference to the life of someone else. Not all second hand clothes income goes to charity of course, but whether the proceeds go to a charity, a business, or an individual, the fact that it's all recycling can only be a good thing.

LESS FASHION DICTATION

One of the main reasons I give for shopping second hand is rather strangely that you'll find less of a fashion season influence. This might seem strange, but what you find is that if (for example) red is this season's must have colour, you tend to find it everywhere on the high street, to the exclusion of the other colours of the rainbow. By shopping second hand you will often find you have more choice available for your own colours and body shape.

QUALITY

I find that the quality of second hand clothes these days is excellent – many items still have the labels on! In my dress agency, I am frequently given clothes to sell on that still have the (not insubstantial) tags attached – never worn. One day a lovely lady gave me a bin bag that had been in her garage for 2 years – the bag contained 3 pairs of Jimmy Choo shoes, a pair of Prada's and a Louis Vuitton handbag! These items were all in fantastic condition, and by buying them secondhand, you can enjoy amazingly good designer brands for a fraction of the price. It's the ultimate in guilt free shopping!

CLEANING

When I talk to clients about charity shopping, the ones that don't shop second hand always complain of that certain charity shop smell. Nowadays, most charity shops have changed a lot and the odd smelly junk shop is definitely no longer the norm. In fact check out Oxfam in Bath and you think you're walking into a high-end trendy boutique! For anyone who is concerned about the fact that these clothes are pre-loved, I say OK, accept that everything has been worn – the first thing to do when you get it home is to wash it. How often do you wash something brand new from a shop? Never I'm guessing – but where has that fabric been? Through warehouses, shipping, production, more warehouses. Which items are truly cleaner the first time you wear them?

FINANCIAL

The other reasons for shopping second hand is about cost per wear. I ask my clients - how often are you going to wear this? If it's going to be a one off occasion - for example an evening dress, then it can seem a lot to go to the shops and spend over £100 on one outfit that you'll probably only wear one or two times. Buying second-hand means the cost per wear comes right down to a level to leave you smiling. The other huge financial benefit is how much you can save in the course of a year. I regularly pick up clothes now for anything between 50p and £20 per item – those same items would cost ten, twenty, even thirty times that new, so I know I'm saving even when I'm buying! I frequently show people how they can practically get a whole new second hand wardrobe for less than £100. The last wedding I went to, I wore shoes and a coat from my wardrobe, and a lace dress I bought for £4. The only other thing I bought was a new pair of tights, which were more than the dress! I spent a total of £8.99 on that outfit, and I felt marvelous in it.

UNIQUE

The other reason to embrace second hand style is about helping you to dress in an individual way. There's nothing worse than heading to a party and finding you're wearing the same dress as someone else. Mixing it up from charity shops ensures this won't happen.

CHOICE

You might think that by shopping second hand, you won't have as much choice as is available to you on the high street. Firstly, I'm not sure that choice is exactly a good thing, especially when it comes to clothes. Too much choice lends for a confusing and time consuming shopping trip. I'm much more a fan of 'try it on, if it fits you, suits you and works for your rules, then buy it; if not, leave it'. Don't try on eight pairs of navy trousers, only to go back and buy the ones you tried on first. These days, and with the quality of second hand clothes being so good, there is plenty of choice, as long as you know where to look. Just go on to eBay and type in some of your favourite labels to see how much second hand choice is available, or have a look at http://www.oxfam.org.uk/shop/womens-clothing.

PITFALLS

So, there's the good stuff, the nice meaty reasons to give second hand shopping a go. But you also need to be armed with the things to watch out for, the mistakes and traps I've discovered along the way that need to be avoided.

OVER-EXCITEMENT

We've all seen people that shop secondhand and they look like they're wearing everything they own. Clashing prints, clothes often too big, the odd inappropriate shoulder pad can all give the game away. This is perhaps someone who has fallen head over heels in love with charity shopping and gorged on the endeavor without any thought or planning. If you go out charity shopping with no idea of the image you want to create for yourself, guess what? The price, the bargains will lure you in to buying things that just don't suit you, or worse, things that are ludicrous on you in the name of being individual. Please don't do that. Go out with your game plan, and stick to it.

PRICE

The price of the clothes can be second hand shopping's biggest pitfall. Many times I've scooped up armloads of jumble because everything's 20p, only to get home and realize I have spent £2 on a bag full of rubbish I'll never wear. That doesn't help anyone. It just means you bag it all up and send it on to the next charity jumble, or stuff it into your already overcrowded wardrobe with a vague idea that you might wear it one day. All we have then is a storage problem. Tempting as it is, don't be lured by the price – before you buy anything, make sure it's something you like and you'll wear.

MAKING OUTFITS

Buying second hand also means you don't have those beautifully merchandised department store systems in place to helpfully show you that this top goes with these trousers, and oh, here's a bag that just happens to match perfectly and oh wow, might as well get a cardigan too. None of that, no, if you're lucky a second hand shop might be arranged in colour groups, or size order, but beyond that there's little merchandising and therefore a danger that you'll end up with a top that no matter how much you love it, just doesn't go with anything else you've got at home. Or you find some green shoes, and then have no clue what to wear them with. To avoid a disparate, mismatched wardrobe, understanding your own set of colours that suits you will really help you to pull together a wardrobe made up of seemingly individual pieces.

ONE-OFFS

There's nothing more annoying than finding something you absolutely love, only to discover it's a size 8. No amount of squeezing my ribcage together or breathing in will get me into a size 8. We just have to accept that in the second hand world, that's the way it is. There will be times you'll love something and it won't be in your size. Do not be tempted to buy it any way with the idea that you'll slim into it. Unless you can wear it now, you're not to give it a home. Buying things that don't fit means they take up space. The only caveat to this is if you're skilled on a machine and you buy something that needs some simple alterations or taking in slightly, or taking up. But please, only buy it if you're actually going to then do the work needed. Remember, unworn clothes just become rags in our wardrobe and these clothes deserve better.

GOLD PANNING

I'm going to sound like a budgie now. Just clock how many times I say 'cheap".

Second hand shopping is cheap, but you need to avoid it being cheap. When I go charity shopping, I would say that at least 50% of the rails (probably more) is full of clothes that were cheap in the first place. Supermarket brands, cheap high street stores and stuff that looks like it came from a budget market stall is a complete waste of your money as a second hand treasure hunter. These are rarely treasures as they were cheaply made initially, and they may end up costing not much less to buy second hand. Threads and buttons are likely to unravel, jumpers to bobble, and manmade fabrics will always look just that. Badly cut design and poor quality fabrics is not what this is about. We are hunting for treasure and I'm afraid you're going to have to sift through quite a lot of these pebbles in order to find the gold.

Budgie rant over. Nine Cheaps.

BUILDING A FOUNDATION

Even if you're a dedicated eco- warrior, you won't find everything you want in charity shops. That's a fact that I've learned along the way. There are still things you'll have to buy new, even if you do brush your teeth with moss and recycle your own hair into rugs. Underwear, swimwear, nightwear; those things I think are a given. Even sportswear I wouldn't buy secondhand unless it was brand new, and some people wouldn't even put their foot in a second hand shoe. But there are other things that underpin a wardrobe that you just can't get in any decent quality second hand. I know, because I've looked. Things like leggings, vest tops, t-shirts. It's often these jersey fabrics that suffer from use and end up worn and misshapen. Often they just don't look nice enough to sell on when they get to the charity shop and are recycled.

Don't feel you have to buy your whole wardrobe from charity shops because otherwise you'll probably not get started. Accepting that there are a few basics you'll need, and you can top up from there is a brilliant start point for anyone. What I've found is that I really treasure and look after those things I've bought new – they are treated really well by me, I look after them and choose them very carefully as so little of my wardrobe is new that those items feel special. I buy nice underwear and nightwear, good quality swimwear and a few key jersey basics. These come from Kettlewell (www.kettlewellcolours.co.uk) and I recommend them to my clients too – partly because they have such a great colour choice, partly because I know they wash well and last well, and partly because I like all the photos they post on their website about their production factory in Turkey.

So, there we are. Laid bare. You now know the good and the bad, but don't head off to the shops just yet. What you need first is a game plan.

CHAPTER 4: YOUR GAME PLAN

How to create a useful second hand wardrobe

Creating any wardrobe requires a bit of thought in advance. Believe me, I've seen plenty of wardrobes that have had no thought or planning put into them, and you don't want to be in that place. Creating a second hand wardrobe requires a bit of specialist planning, because you just can't plan for what you might find. So, how do you plan for something you can't plan for?

In my experience, not many second hand shopping trips are predictable. I might go looking for a dress to wear to a wedding and find instead an amazing coat. One day I might spend hours hunting and come home empty handed (rare), or pop out for half an hour and find four or five fab things. It's all just a bit hit and miss, and part of the fun and appeal of charity shopping is that you never quite know what you're going to find.

So, if you regularly charity shop and don't know quite what you'll come home with, how do you stop your own wardrobe turning into a mish mash collection of random treasures that don't actually go or work together? How can you create a collection of clothes that makes sense from a completely brilliant yet random series of shopping expeditions? And how can you stop yourself just buying more and hoping it will all somehow work? Unless you're a very creative dresser (and plenty I know are – you can usually spot them by their pink hair, clashing prints, and lemon yellow duffel coat – yes, you know who you are), you'll want to bring a bit of law and order to your wardrobe to stop it getting out of control. So, before we let you loose in your local Cancer Research, lets start with some practical ways to build a wardrobe collection that actually works for you. If you go off blindly into the world of charity shopping, you'll find so many bargains, that you'll need to move house to accommodate it all, and that just won't do. I don't want you to have MORE clothes, but I do want you to love the hell out of the clothes you have and will find on your expeditions. In this chapter, we'll be exploring the rules we need to set up around our wardrobe to make sure it works for you and your lifestyle. In fact, let's start just there, with you.

Think about your life for a moment. Forget about the time you're actually asleep and focus on what you do during waking hours on a typical week. How would you break your time down to specific activities? If you mapped out your week on a pie chart, what would it look like? What percentage of your time is spent at work? At home? Out socially? Engaged in a hobby or activity? Now think about the clothes you wear for each activity – maybe work and home merge because you happen to work from home. Maybe work needs to be broken down more because you need clothes for travel, meeting clients, giving presentations, and dress down Fridays? Perhaps your hobbies are going to the gym and an evening class in creative writing – two very different styles of clothes needed in your hobby category then. Break your life down into what you need to wear for different occasions and how much time you spend in each of these different roles. Here's an example of one of my clients charts:

Sue's Lifestyle Diagrams:

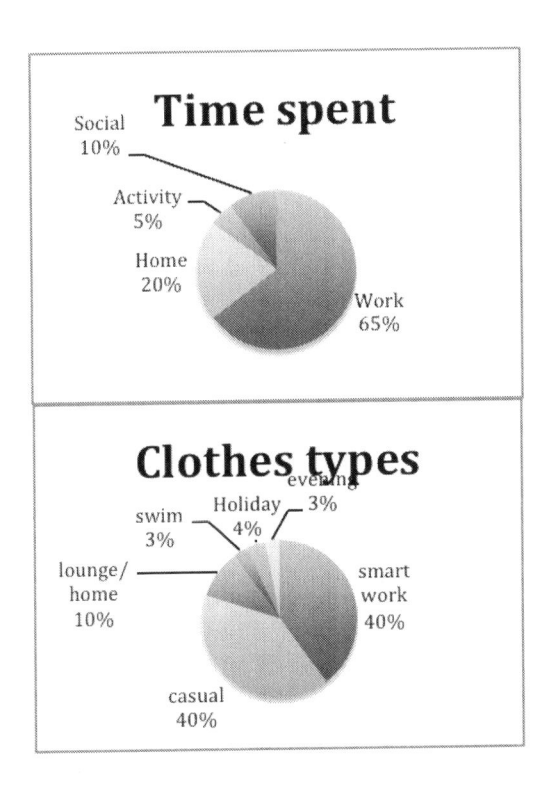

Time spent
- Social 10%
- Activity 5%
- Home 20%
- Work 65%

Clothes types
- evening 3%
- Holiday 3%
- swim 3%
- lounge/home 10%
- smart work 40%
- casual 40%

Sue could split up her week easily enough, but when we looked more closely at what clothes she actually needed to wear for each of the different activities, we found that there was a definite difference between her client facing days and dress down Fridays at work. This dramatically increased the amount of time she spent in more casual clothes. When we looked in Sue's wardrobe we realized that nowhere near 40% of her wardrobe was dedicated to casual wear. We also found that she had been keeping all her evening and occasion wear (some of which no longer fitted her) and that this category was way more than 3% of her wardrobe space. Whilst talking about her lifestyle, Sue also revealed that she loved to go and visit her mum in Spain, so we added in an allowance for hot destination holidays in her activity category.

This exercise is really useful as it helps you to identify if you wardrobe is really doing its job of fulfilling all of the roles you have in life, or if there are any gaps. A lot of people have a wardrobe full of clothes but often a large chunk of it is no use whatsoever because it's not relevant to their current roles or lifestyle. What we don't want to do here is give you full permission to go charity shopping because chances are you'll be in the same buying patterns and will end up buying more of the things you don't need. We have to be disciplined to only go looking for the kind of things you know you are going to wear, love wearing, and wear a lot. So, start here, and let's start breaking down your wardrobe and your lifestyle. Start by working out how much of your time is spent in the different roles in your life. How much of your time is spent at work, at home, in a hobby or out socially? Are there other roles in your life that you spend a proportion of your time doing? Write them out and give them a percentage score. Now, think about the different clothes you need to wear in each of these roles – do some roles merge into others, or are they very distinctive? Like Sue, you may have clothes for some or all of the following categories:

Work wear - (Uniform, Smart, or Smart Casual)

Casual wear - (For work, daywear, daytime socializing, school runs or everyday)

Home clothes - (For cleaning, gardening, lounging, home based activities, watching TV, stroking the cat)

Evening wear - (For going out socially, for parties, balls, or just down the pub)

Activity wear - (For sports, specific hobbies or interests)

Anything else - (holiday wear, ski wear, Christmas jumpers etc)

There are two schools of thought here. One is that the more your roles can merge, the better. That means you'll be choosing clothes for you, that you love, and that you can wear in multiple areas of your life. A smaller wardrobe is possible, it would be more cohesive, and you'll be choosing things you can dress up or down with some simple accessories. The other school of thought is that we sometimes need to be or feel different in different areas of our lives. You might have a stressful managerial role at work where you're required to bring out the authoritarian in you, but at home, you might just want to flop on the sofa with a hot chocolate and a slushy rom-com? Completely different outfits are required. Some people even find that putting on that suit for work helps them get into the role quicker, almost like putting on a superhero costume. It's still you in the boss/ hot chocolate scenario; just different aspects of you need to come to the fore at different times. Clothes can help you define and separate the different roles you have. Have a think about these two approaches and decide which is right for you.

When I first went to a stylist, I had two very different

wardrobes – a corporate suit wardrobe and a stay and home and don't mind if I get thrown up on mummy wardrobe. The two never met, and the stylist suggested that if I upgrade my mummy wardrobe and soften my corporate wardrobe, that I could start to buy things that I could enjoy wearing in both roles, dressed up or down. For a while this approach was a total revelation to me, and certainly helped me to learn to choose clothes that I loved rather than thought might be 'useful' for work or home life. My wardrobe really started to reflect me, and I felt better in my home life and more authentic in my working life. Over time, however, and as I've gotten more confident, I find I do very subtly shift my wardrobe to different roles. I do have more things that cross over, but equally if a client is coming, I move to a handful of favourite outfits that I know work well for me when I'm meeting someone new. I also found that by wearing my clothes all the time, I was getting bleach marks or cooking stains on my favourite jumpers, or snagging a lovely skirt while out with the dogs or at the park with the kids. I've got a collection of clothes now that I can chuck on and I don't mind what happens to them – I can garden, clean and dog walk in them and it's OK, but they're not necessarily things I'd meet a client in, even though everything I wear reflects an aspect of me.

Deciding what you need for your lifestyle and how much you're willing to let the lines blur between your roles is a great first step. Have a quick look through your current wardrobe and see how close you are to your pie charts in terms of what you currently own. Do you notice any areas where you've bought far more than you actually need? How about the gaps? Where do you not quite have enough for the amount of time you spend in that role?

Quite often, this exercise will uncover buying patterns. A buying pattern is where you've bought something, and felt particular pleasure in the purchase – perhaps you were complimented when you wore it, or especially loved the item. Next time you go shopping, your mind will want to give you the same kind of euphoric feeling, so it will look for things that could replicate that for you, and often you'll end up coming home with something very similar. One of my clients had just such a pattern with black trousers. When we uncovered every pair she owned we found that she had bought 73 pairs. Your pattern might not be quite that extreme, but think about whether you have any unconscious buying patterns going on, and resolve to break them. Usually just being aware of them is enough to stop them resurfacing.

The single biggest (and quickest and easiest) way to build a wardrobe that makes sense is by using colour. Not only that, but colour can affect the way you look and the way you feel. By sticking to a palette of colours, you can create a fairly small wardrobe, but everything in it goes together so the number of possible outfits is huge. Think about it for a minute – if you stuck to a colour palette of soft pinks and blues, and used grey or navy as your base colour, every item you owned would work together, wouldn't it? I'm not suggesting we all go out and buy baby pink, it's just to give you an example.

Now, because I am a personal stylist, I'm of course going to tell you that the best way of finding out which colour palette is right for you is by going to see someone like me for a colour analysis. It might be an upfront cost, but I promise you that in the long run you'll get that money back in savings (and more besides). Knowing your colour palette saves you buckets of time and money.

When I work with a client on colour, there are four possible colour palettes we can explore, and picking the right one is dependent on the undertones in the skin, hair and eyes of my client. Each palette has a set of base colours, colours that underpin everything – they're the colours that work for shoes, trousers, skirts, that kind of thing. Even if you haven't had your colours done, understanding how a palette works and which types of colours go together is really valuable for putting a wardrobe together.

There's another reason why understanding colour is such a good thing to do, and that's what the right colours can do for you. My clients tell me over and over again that when they start wearing the tones of colours that are right for them, they get compliments. People notice how great they look, and can't always put their finger on why. One lady had a work colleague guessing every possible scenario; have you had your hair done? No. Have you been on holiday? No. Have you had Botox? No. You get the idea. Simply by choosing tones of colours that marry up and amplify the natural tones in our skin, hair and eyes, you can look hands down wonderful.

When I run colour consultations, there are four colour palettes that each share something special about their tones, and we each look best in one of these four groups. The colour groups are named after the four seasons, and each season reflects something about those colours;

Winter; Deep, cool, bright, clear jewel-like dramatic colours that are full of energy – these are colours to get you noticed!

Winter colours examples: Base colours: Black, White, Charcoal, Navy. Accent Colours: Fuchsia, Cobalt Blue, Emerald Green, Purple

Spring; Bright, warm, light clear fun colours that are happy and creative – these are colours that make your eyes sparkle!

Spring colour examples: Base colours: Navy, Cream, Tan, Bright Blue. Accent Colours: Mango, Coral, Apple Green, Buttercup Yellow

Summer; Soft, cool, light gentle tones that subtly blend beautifully and elegantly together – these are calm, beautiful, summer garden colours.

Summer colour examples: Base colours: Navy, Grey, White, Blue-Grey. Accent Colours: Soft Pink, Baby Blue, Lavender, Sage Green

Autumn; Warm, deep, muted colours that reflect the colours of nature – these colours are earthy, spicy colours like an autumn countryside.

Autumn colour examples: Base colours: Brown, Cream, Olive, Marine Navy. Accent Colours: Warm red, Orange, Teal Blue, Khaki Green

Have a look at the descriptions of colour groups above, and see if there is a group of colours that you feel most drawn to. Each palette is designed to work together, so in each group you have base colours (these are for things that everything else needs to go with, so things like shoes, boots, maybe trousers, coats – that kind of thing) and you have accent colours (these are the exciting colours that each works with the base colours beautifully and look great as tops, dresses, jewellery, or splashes of colour on your outfit). So, if you're thinking of putting outfits together, can you see how much easier it would be if you had a palette of colours to stick to? Of course it is! You'll never have that odd top hanging at the end of the wardrobe again (you know, the one you bought in the Debenhams sale, but the tag is still on it because it just doesn't GO with anything). To see a full range of colours for each season, have a look at the brilliant website for Kettlewell (www.kettlewellcolours.co.uk) and click on the 'Shop by Colour' tab to see colours for each season.

What exciting wardrobes they'd be! Can you imagine opening the doors of each of these wardrobes, and seeing how beautifully the colours go together in each? Now imagine one of those wardrobes is yours, which one do you think you'd be?

Now we come on to talk about wardrobe basics. There are some things in a wardrobe that most people need to have. Things that underpin everything else. Wardrobe basics are things like camisole tops, vest tops, t-shirts, leggings – usually things that are made of a jersey type fabric. I've found that these things aren't readily available from second hand sources. Inevitably there will be some things that you'll just have to buy new. Underwear (yes, of course), tights, socks, and also those key basics that you just can't get second hand.

Think about your basics as foundations that your amazing new house of style will be built on – get the basics right and the rest of the project is ten times easier. I don't include jeans as basics – believe it or not, jeans are not for everyone, even though most of us seem to be born in a pair of jeans, they just don't work for some people. Jeans are definitely a choice rather than an essential, but if you choose that you love your denim so much they have to always have a part to play in your wardrobe, then include them in the list by all means. Basics I would recommend are; camisole or vest tops, t-shirts, leggings, long sleeved tops for layering, soft lounge trousers, underwear and nightwear. Have a look in your wardrobe and see if you have enough basics to get you started. If not, think about adding this to your shopping list and look for some basics in your chosen colour palette.

When it comes to flexibility, you'd be hard pushed to find a more economical way of adding a multitude of options to your wardrobe than accessorizing. A necklace over a simple t-shirt turns it into something else. A great pair of shoes transforms leggings. Using accessories will help you to build outfits and add colour, fun, drama and focal points to what you wear. Have a think about the kind of accessories you like to wear. It might be necklaces; it might be bracelets, rings or earrings. You might have a particular fondness for sniffing the leather on a handbag (anyone? OK, maybe that's just me then) or you might love a belt. Many people who are winter colouring have a special place in their hearts reserved only for shoes. Hats or glasses are rarer passions but no less valid. Think about what you like to wear, and remember that accessories act as focal points – these laser beam other peoples attention to that part of your body, so be prepared for people to notice it. Belt look amazing on hourglass shapes who curve dramatically in at the waist for example. Awesome shoes are going to get your ankles noticed, and necklaces and earrings will draw the eye up to your face. Think about what you love to wear, where you want to draw attention, and then add a small collection of those accessories to your shopping list.

I'm going to give you a golden rule that trumps all other rules of colour, shape and style. Are you ready? That rule is that we always look our best when we wear colours, shapes and styles that reflect the best of our natural self. So, we look incredible when we wear colours in line with our own tones, shapes that reflect our natural body shape, and styles that say something about who we are and our personality.

We're going to spend just a moment focused on your shape. This is important because it will help you to understand why some things work and some things don't. Why your friend looks incredible in that 50's prom dress but on you it's more like the sugar plum fairy. It's because of your shape. When we look at shape, we look at your skeleton, so for a moment, I want you to imagine you can see your skeleton, like looking at an airport X-ray machine.

If you're a lady, you'll have one of two types of skeletal frame, a straight one or a curved one. A curved one might mean that your shoulders have a slight slope to them, you might have pronounced hips, but the curve in your ribcage allows your waist to go in at the middle. If you're straight shaped you'll have straight shoulders, straight or long curved hips, and your ribcage will be straight, meaning you simply don't go in and out in the middle as much as your curvy cousins. To find out, have a look in a full-length mirror. Grab a broom or a mop, anything with a long handle, and hold it against your shoulder and hip. Now, how big is the gap between your waist and the stick? More than 3 fingers or less? If it's more than 3 fingers chances are you've a curve in your ribcage, any less and your ribcage is probably straight.

What this means is that curvy ladies benefit from wearing clothes that show off the waist. They suit fabrics that gently follow the curve of the body, they look good in curvy patterns or prints with movement, round necks and curvy details. Jeans are a real bugbear to curvy girls, as the stiff denim fabric doesn't allow for the curves on her body.

Straighter framed ladies need clothes that are straighter. Trousers always work well, straight skirts, collars, jackets, and fabrics that are straighter and more structured. Straighter details, zip, V-necks, stripes, checks and straight lines work well on straight framed ladies.

There's a lot more involved to understand your body shape but as we are all so individual and unique, it's impossible to share it in a way that makes sense to everyone. This ready reckoner means at least you can get started in finding things that suit your frame, and that's a fantastic starting point. If you've got a taste for wanting to know more about shape, find a good local image consultant to help you.

Right, time for a quiz. Bono's glasses, Springsteens jeans, Mrs Thatchers handbags. What do these three things have in common?

The wearer is rarely seen without them, in fact I can't look at an open neck white shirt without thinking of Simon Cowell. These style statements have become so much a part of the wearer that they are forever linked. Have you got a style signature?

When I went to see an image consultant, one of the things

she suggested to me was to wear cowboy boots. Cowboy boots, I admit don't appeal to everyone, however her suggestion to me was something of a revelation. The idea of putting on a pair of cowboy boots really clicked with me. I love the idea of dressing in a relaxed casual way, and adding in an element of the unusual. I'm also, because I am my mother's daughter, quite partial to a bit of country and western music, and I love horse riding. Of course it makes complete sense to me that a pair of cowboy boots fits with my image of myself (and not in a line dancing, how-dee kind of way). They're also extremely comfortable.

Think about you and your life for a moment. What do you love? What matters to you? What can you introduce to your wardrobe to make it feel unique and exciting to you? Perhaps you have a love of bright coats or jackets, maybe it's hand made earrings. Perhaps your penchant is for pearls, or maybe you have an unexplored love of interesting buttons. Bright and sparkly things work for some, whereas others might prefer something that has a natural element (think wooden pendants, or prints that reflect animals or nature). Perhaps you love bright floral prints, or dots, or scarves, or brooches. Whatever it is you love, indulge it and make it part of you. That's how we create a wardrobe that's all about you and that you love, rather than something that feels simply 'useful' and generic (which I can guarantee you over time will become boring to you – that's when you stop enjoying clothes – if you've been there already you'll know just what I mean).

If you've been in a dark place for a long time, chances are you won't even know what you like anymore. One thing you might like to try is to look back through old photographs and create a history timeline of outfits you've worn and loved in your life. It's fun to look back at the styles and see what worked, and what didn't. It might trigger a memory of a dress you loved, or a favourite print. You wouldn't necessarily choose those styles again but it will help to reconnect you to the idea of loving and enjoying your clothes again.

One thing I had as a child was a red cotton dress. I have no memory of where it came from (handed down I guess) but this dress was special because it was red and had parrots all over it. It also had a matching bolero jacket which I thought was super fancy – I felt like a princess in it. I remember my grandparents taking me to Rode Bird Gardens to see the parrots in my parrot dress, which I was very excited about. Connecting with how you felt in something you loved helps to remind us what special clothes can feel like and do for us again.

One of the things I enjoy doing when I have a spare five minutes and a steaming mug of coffee by my side, is to see what others have created on Pinterest. Getting dressed is a visual process – we are working towards how we look and how others see us, so getting inspiration is also a visual process – we need pictures.

When I work with clients on style and shape, one of the things I always recommend they do is to piece together their own style board. A style board is simply a place where you can put all the ideas and images you love. When you put it all together, it's much easier to spot trends and ideas popping up, and also to get an idea of where you're heading, or how many different images make up your idea of you. Pinterest is a good place for creating a style board, but I also like using Polyvore (www.polyvore.com). Simply drag and drop clothes and accessories you like the look of and you can start to piece together your very own style board. Mine started with a pair of cowboy boots and worked out from there. In a year's time, I'll do another one, just to keep in touch with my style board and any changes that may have happened during my last year. If you want to have a look and see my board, go to polyvore.com/my_style_board_2015/set?id=157704834.

For the ladies among us who still need a fashion fix (or who have decided that looking fashionable and up to date is a key part of their style, image and identity), then please don't give up on second hand. By all means visit the high street (without your credit card) for ideas and inspiration. The high street will tell you what's in right now. Fashion magazines will tell you what's coming – they're another great source of ideas. You can see what the designers are sending down the catwalk for the autumn, and be looking for similar ideas in charity shops now. I guarantee you'll find it, or close to it.

As you've worked through the suggestions and wardrobe audit recommended in this chapter, you've hopefully been jotting down some ideas and a shopping list of the kind of things you need. Decide on your colour palette, or go and see a trained consultant to help determine your colours, and get some understanding of your own body shape. Figure out what you love, and find inspiration for styles and outfits online. Make sure you have your wardrobe basics in place, and you should be ready with your game plan of what to look for at the shops.

Now, where are you going to go exactly?

CHAPTER 5: GETTING OUT THERE

How to shop second hand and get the most out of it

Buying pre-loved clothes doesn't just mean popping down to your local British Heart Foundation and having a quick rummage through the jumpers. There are loads of different ways you can find and buy second hand clothing, I've tried them all and can safely say that some dig up more treasure than others. Some, like the jumble sale, are really for the more intrepid hunter, whilst finding a good local dress agency will feel just like walking into a high-end boutique and is usually a great place to start.

Most people's idea of turfing up a bargain comes from charity shopping (or thrift store shopping for our friends across the pond). If you live in or near a town, I can guarantee you'll have a charity shop or two near you. There's a handy link to find some of the charity shops in your area http://www.charityretail.org.uk/find-a-charity-shop/. The main exciting advantage with charity shopping is that you never know what you'll find as the stock is updated several times a day, so if you went in yesterday, chances are there will be different pieces in there today. It's a never-ending source of fun.

Nowadays a lot of charity shops have sorted their clothes by type and colour so it's easy to see what you're looking for. My local Cancer Research shop is a pleasure to browse around. The other thing I love about charity shops is that they usually have large windows that let in lots of natural light to the shop. Sometimes high street stores, and especially large department stores leave you blinking like a mole or someone who's been in a coma when you finally emerge. Natural light is a more pleasant shopping sensation, and also helps you to see the colours of clothes properly. I've bought many an item in a department store in the past, only to get it home and realize it's not the colour I thought it was at all – what looked like a lovely sage green is actually more baby nappy green in the light. In charity shops, this doesn't happen. There are usually changing rooms in charity shops now, and most will let you take things back if you keep the receipt and the label on it.

If charity shopping still feels like a step too far for you, then I'd recommend you start with a dress agency. Dress agencies will accept clothes from clients, which they then sell on their behalf, usually splitting the income 50/50. This means that what you tend to find in dress agencies are clothes that people have spent a lot of money on originally, or clothes that are still new with the labels on, and the owners are hoping to recoup a bit of cash for. All the dress agencies I know (my own included) have an admission policy of what they will accept for sale, so it's usually high-end high street, boutique and designer labels only, and they have to be in as new condition. You can expect to pay a lot more than charity shop prices in a dress agency, but still nowhere near what the item would have cost originally. Dress agencies are laid out professionally, and are not usually rammed full of clothes, it's a relaxed shopping experience where you may well find yourself a designer bargain or two. I particularly love Revolution in Henley on Thames and there's one in Totnes called The Loft I walked into thinking it was a beautiful boutique. Type in Dress Agency and the name of your local town in to Google and you'll be able to find one near you. It's a great place to get started in changing your shopping habits to pre-loved, you're very likely to find something beautiful and unusual I too. If you want to wear more designer clothes but can't quite reach the designer price tags, a dress agency is a great place to start looking.

If you're a fan of online shopping, then the biggest second hand shop in the world awaits you; eBay. eBay is wonderful because its open 24/7, you can be very specific in your search of what you want, and because there is so much on there, you're probably going to find it. Just a few clicks and voila, page after page of glorious items to have a look at. And this can be a problem. It's almost too easy to shop on eBay. I have a client who enjoys a bit of late night shopping on eBay after a glass of wine or two, and then can't remember what she's ordered until it arrives. She says it's like Christmas when she opens the parcels because she's genuinely forgotten what's inside. As you can imagine, mixed results.

If you're going to have a look on eBay, start with a really good idea of what you're looking for. Typing in "blue ladies work dress size 14" sounds specific, but, honestly, you'll get hundreds of results to trawl through. I recommend that you pick two or three labels that you love and you know work for your shape, then you can try searching for those, so a more specific search might be "Boden navy blue ladies work dress size 14". I have a client who loves Vivienne Westwood, so I often search for that label to see what's available. A bit like the charity shop, new things are added to eBay all the time, and you can set up alerts to notify you when something new comes online that you're looking for. Put your search terms in the search box, see what comes up, and then click 'follow this search' to get updates on new things that meet your search terms. I recommend this as a good way to keep an eye on your favourite labels.

The downside of using eBay (and all online methods) is that you don't get to see, feel or try the item until it arrives at your home. Sellers are required to post photographs and give a detailed description of the quality of an item and any defects, but to be safe, only buy from sellers who accept returns. At least then if it arrives and you're not happy, you can send it back. I once ordered a silk Noli dress on eBay for a party. The seller had described it well, but when it came, some past owner had hand sewn the neckline together, which I had to unpick to get it on, leaving marks in the silk. I'd paid £45 for the dress, which is quite a bit in the second hand world, so I was disappointed with this one. On the other hand, I picked up a marvellous pair of L K Bennett shoes for £4.99, which the owner said were being sold cheap because they were badly scratched. When I got them, the scratches were hardly noticeable, and I was delighted with them. Don't be afraid to ask the seller questions before you commit to buying something if you're not sure of the condition, the colour or the quality. I sell regularly on eBay for my dress agency and people are always messaging me asking me to measure various unusual parts of the garment, which I'm always very happy to do.

If you buy something on eBay that you're really pleased with you can mark the seller as a favourite, then you can search your favourite sellers to see what they're selling at the moment. I once bought a beautiful Kew floral duster coat from a lady for £35. It arrived packaged in tissue paper by next day post and was exactly as described and photographed. I instantly made the seller one of my favourites, and found that she sold quite a bit of Kew and Jigsaw stuff, which I liked. It's a great way to keep track of sellers that you know are reliable and deliver good quality items.

Of course there's not just eBay online where you can shop second hand. There are literally hundreds of other sites. Even on Facebook there are local groups that buy and sell and there are plenty of clothes sellers on there, usually selling things in lots. I quite like looking at Preloved but I do find I get waylaid with things like vintage armchairs and old sideboards when I'm looking. One of the sites I really enjoy is the Oxfam online website http://www.oxfam.org.uk/shop. I can spend many a happy moment browsing the online vintage section. The search facility is great, it just feels like a regular online shop. I also like the fact that in the vintage section, you can shop by decade, or by fabric as well as the other regular search facilities – it's a great website to start a bit of an online browsing addiction. If online shopping really isn't your thing and you prefer the cut and thrust of physically being there and having a good old rummage, then look no further than the jumble sale.

When I was small, and I used to go to Jumble sales with my Nan, they were easy shopping territory for me. I could slip unseen through the throng of elbows and make my way to the front. Oh to have that skill again. So unless Harry Potter lends me his cloak of invisibility, as an adult, I have to resign myself to getting stuck in with the rest of them. If you've never been to a jumble sale before, imagine a polite rugby scrum, or the Gary Barlow fan club as he walks into a room. Yes, there's some jostling. Yes, you might get your toe trodden on. You've got to be bold at a jumble sale – this is no time for timidity. Timidity gets you the back of the throng and only able to look at books or bric-a-brac. No, to get to the decent clothes in a jumble sale, you need a place at the front, you need to not mind other peoples elbows in your way, and you need to plant your feet very firmly.

If you go to a sale and the other buyers are old hands, what you find is that a sort of assembly line forms at the jumble. In front of you is a wonky trestle table about to collapse under the weight of about a ton of clothes, and you need to find some treasure in it. That means handling and looking at as much as possible as quickly as possible before it's snapped up by the person who is standing right over your shoulder and ready to pounce. Professional jumble salers take the top item on the pile in front of them, examine it, and move it to the right so that they can look at the next item. The person to their right, then picks up their discarded item, examines it and moves it along, thus creating a sorting system, which means that nearly all unwanted items end up on the right. My advice, start as far left as you can and get sorting. Woe betides the left-handed person at the jumble who sorts from right to left.

As you may have guessed by now, a jumble sale is not in any way rookie territory. You've got to know what you're doing at a jumble sale. It's easy to spot the inexperienced hunter; they don't bring a bag, or try to pay for a 10p top with a £20 note. They wave their arms over the throng and just grab items at random, upsetting the production line system. No ladies, don't do this. If you've never been to a jumble before, go with someone who has, or go knowing that this is how it all works. Get there early, take plenty of loose change, get your place at the table, and just rummage. If you like the look of something, sling it over one arm until either it's too big a pile and you can't hold it anymore, or until you're done and then pay for it all in one go. It sounds like hard work because it is. It is physically demanding and not for the claustrophobe, but most jumbles helpfully put on a tea and cake stall so you can revive yourself before going in for round two. I recommend going round everything twice, because there is just so much stuff at a jumble, you're bound to miss something the first time around.

I can hear you now.

You're saying, Oh my god, V, is it worth putting yourself through all this? Why on earth would you do that? And I would say to you, because it's really good fun! Honestly. I love the way it works, and the firm but polite old ladies who fiercely guard their space. I love the thrill of not knowing what I'm going to find and the fact it's all in a pile, just waiting to be discovered. I love the people who run the jumbles who are always smiling, armed with dozens of old plastic bags for anyone who turns up without one.

My favourite jumble sale is one held twice a year in the village where we go on holiday. And, what do you know; our holidays match the dates of the jumble – what a co-incidence! I always leave this jumble with bags and bags of treasure, and then wish I hadn't walked the mile to get there and brought the car instead. And how much does this most pleasant of past times cost? I've never spent more than £4. £4 was a mother lode of a haul from this jumble sale. Most items are 10p or 20p, and the most I've paid in a jumble for an item of clothing was 50p. It's cheap as chips. Yes, it is a jumble so there are no rules on quality. You've got to wade through holey jumpers and bobbly skirts to find your treasure, but let me promise you – treasure is there! I've bought a beautiful cream Hobbs cardigan (10p), a white stuff top (10p), a lovely floral M&S skirt (10p), a designer merino wrap (20p), and a red leather M&S handbag (10p) to name but just a few items from jumble sales. If you've the constitution of a Jane Austen character, jumbles are not for you, but if you're strong and brave and you love a bargain, dive in my friends, elbows first.

There's no online directory for jumbles, but start with the what's on listings for your local paper, or look round local church halls. Most jumbles are advertised with A4 posters stuck to lampposts or put up in the local shop, so start digging around your area, and you're bound to stumble on a jumble sooner or later. Often the same jumble will be held at the same time each year, so check with the organizers when the next one is on.

Another possible source for your new hobby is the car boot sale. I don't see as many car boot sales in my area as I used to, I don't know about you. Maybe I'm just not up and about early enough on a Sunday morning. The thing I love most about car boot sales is seeing what people have tucked under their arms on the trek across the rutted muddy field back to their car. I've bought a dolls house before (that was a challenge) and I've seen people buy lawnmowers, climbing frames, even once an inflatable crocodile.

IN THE JUMBLE

If you've ever read the Enid Blyton book "The Faraway Tree", you'll know that in it there's the land of take what you want, where the characters wander round and find everything they could possibly want. I'm sure Enid must have been to a car boot or two in her time to inspire this story, or perhaps she inadvertently invented the idea of the car boot sale. You can literally find anything you want at a car boot sale. I've even see people sell the car they've arrived in (although I'm not sure how they get all their unsold stuff or themselves home afterwards).

Car boots are a pleasant enough way to spend an early weekend morning. I guarantee you'll get some great books, maybe even a foot spa, certainly a few heavily loved Barbie's along the way. But when it comes to clothes, I usually find that a car boot can be slim pickings. By the time you've walked end-to-end of a fairly decent sized sale, you've probably covered about nine miles, and all that looking can be exhausting. Clothes sellers are spread out, and most people will be selling clothes alongside a table full of bric-a-brac, so you've got to spot a wobbly rail at the end of someone's table. Because the clothes have had to be transported, don't expect them to be ironed or sorted, or have prices on. Don't necessarily even expect them to be hung up: sometimes clothes are thrown in a pile on a tarpaulin.

In my experience, I've never found a really incredible bargain at a car boot sale. Except one pair of £3 cowboy boots that I wore to death, that's been it. They're not my favourite source of second hand clothes, because you a) have to get up very early, b) have to walk across farmers fields, dodging the cow pats to even get there, c) have to traipse up and down row upon row of men who've been told to clear out their shed or else d) it's often in summer so usually hot and sweaty hunting e) clothes are brought along almost as an afterthought and stuck on the side of a trestle table covered in some child's unwanted toys and books and f) because you're buying directly from the owner, the prices vary hugely. Some just want to get rid of stuff and charge next to nothing, and at the next stall the owner might still have an emotional attachment or guilt over the original price of the item and charge ten times more. There never seems to be an average price at a car boot sale and there's no benchmark on what to charge.

Have you been to a swapping party? Swapping (or swishing) is an incredibly fun way to find some lovely new to you clothes, and it has nothing to do with throwing your car keys onto the coffee table and throwing caution to the wind with someone else's husband. A good swapping event is the ultimate in clothes recycling because you go armed with things that you don't want from your own wardrobe, and bring home a bag of things you do want from someone else's. The idea is that you swap things you don't want any more with someone else. A well-organized swapping party can be a fun social event. You don't even have to wait for someone else to organize one, get your friends together and hold your own. So, how do you go about organizing your own swishing event? Well, firstly you need to set the date and time, and decide who to invite. You can make it a fun weekend evening event or organize one during lunch breaks at work – it's up to you and your guests. Obviously the more people you invite, the more stock you'll have, which is good. If you're inviting men, make sure you invite a few, you don't want one poor lone chap turning up and having no one to swap with. It's quite easy to set up events on Facebook and you can keep in contact with your invitees to remind them nearer the date. You also need to make sure your guests are aware of the swishing rules and what you want them to bring along.

You could hold your event at home, or at work, or if you want to make it bigger, you could hire a local hall (which will probably charge you). How you organize the event can be as simple or as complex as you choose it to be, but one way I've found works well is as follows:

Ask everyone to bring along clothes they no longer wear in advance of the party. Display them nicely and then when the swish officially opens, all the guests can pick whatever they like to try on and take away. If your guests bring along an item of high quality (i.e. designer, or nearly new), display these items in a separate room or area (call it the VIP room or something), and give the guest a token for each item they bring. They can then 'spend' this token on any other item from the VIP area. This way, you get a broad range of clothing types and everyone goes home with something. It's also fair as you've got a system in place for swapping the higher end items.

You can ask your guests to bring along drinks and nibbles to share the cost of any catering, and you will need to provide a large mirror and a changing area for people to try things on. If you want to hang things up, ask friends to bring rails and bring their items on hangers, or if you're going to display on tables and in piles, borrow a few trestles and set them up. I tend to have the majority of stock in piles on the tables, and then the 'VIP' stock hung up on rails. At the end of the swish you can all agree to bag up what's left and donate it to charity, or you could hold a second event and have a refashion and up-cycle party to make new things from the unwanted items. This is very creative and great fun, and you'll have loads of stock to choose from with your swish leftovers! Have a look at the brilliant refashioning ideas on the website www.loveyourclothes.org.uk.

If you get really into your second hand shopping life, you might like to try your hand at vintage. Buying vintage is a specialist past time, and buying true vintage can be the ultimate in treasure hunting. If you have a vintage shop near you, I strongly encourage you to go and check it out (go on, go!). You can almost see the history emanating from the clothes. I love imagining who bought and wore those clothes, where they wore them, and what sort of a person they were. You can build amazing stories around your vintage finds. Personally I find that vintage clothing doesn't really suit me. I'm quite a straight body shape, and a lot of vintage styles have a defined (and alarmingly small) waist, which doesn't look right on me at all. So the 50's is out for me. And most of the 40's. I've got twenties flapper girl or seventies hippy available to me and my shape. That's good news as they're my favourites. I love a pair of good flares, and the straight shapes of the 20's with a bit of sparkle and fringing thrown in, who wouldn't love that?

If you go to a good vintage shop near you, chances are that the person who runs the shop is often also the buyer of the stock. They know a thing or two about vintage, and they can help steer you to some finds that will work for you. Vintage works well if it's mixed up with some more modern styles, and your vintage seller will not only help you choose something, but show you how to wear it too. My favourite vintage shop is a little place at the top of the high street in Totnes. `The last time I was there I spotted the most beautiful silk kimono (which I wish I'd bought and didn't). What struck me most was one room at the back, which was full of vintage wedding dresses. These dresses were beautiful and I almost cried thinking of all the women who wore them on their special day.

I loved watching Dawn Porters "This old thing" on Channel 4, which was a master class in buying and wearing vintage pieces as well as adapting it and mixing it up with what you've already got at home. My favourite vintage find was a checked wool jacket I bought from Bath Flea Market when I was about 17 (shows how long ago that was, as the flea market has been gone for years). It was a 1940's jacket, beautifully made, and cost me about £2. I wore it and wore it and wore it (usually with a pair of Levi's and a polo neck – the polo neck was always a mistake). If I close my eyes now, I can still see the blue buttons on that jacket. I don't remember now what happened to it, I just stopped wearing it and now I don't have it anymore. I miss it like an old friend I've lost contact with. I wish I'd kept it; it was a work of art in itself. If you can find a piece of vintage you love as much as I loved that jacket, you've found real treasure indeed my friend.

As you can see from the last few pages, there are a multitude of places you can buy second hand clothes from. In fact you're probably tripping over second hand clothes sellers on your way to the shops. See which one takes your fancy and give it a try. I'd recommend not necessarily starting online but perhaps finding a good local dress agency or well organized charity shop if this is your first foray into treasure hunting. You need to see and feel the items, try a few things on, learn more about what you like and what you don't before leaping in to the deep end of jumble sales, car boots or online. Start looking around for good locations near you to practice your craft.

If you are planning a treasure hunting trip, think about where would be a good place to go. Lots of people suggest trying the charity shops in wealthy areas to get a designer bargain, but I've not found that to always work. I would always recommend trying places that have at least five shops in a small geographic area – that way you get as much choice as possible in as short a time frame as possible. My friend and I make a regular charity shop journey to Wantage, which is a small but lovely town with lots of charity shops to choose from. We can cover the entire town in a couple of hours, which then gives us time for lunch and a cuppa afterwards, which is just perfect. My sister and I particularly enjoy Devizes, it's in between our homes, has loads of charity shops, and an especially lovely bistro where we stop off for lunch. I also love browsing the charity shops in new places when I go on holiday – you never know what you're going to find! Once you've found a place you like, keep going back and hunting for the items on your list.

In Newbury, we're very lucky. Not only have we got some great charity shops, but we also have a huge clothes recycling centre that's open to the public. It's called the Clothing Warehouse, and I'm regularly in there hunting for treasures for my wardrobe and my client's wardrobes. It's a huge barn that is stuffed full from floor to ceiling with just about every item, type, size and colour of clothes you can imagine. For someone who loves treasure hunting, it's nirvana. For someone who loathes a rummage, it's like having your nails pulled off. Slowly. Knowing your local area, where to go and how to find good second hand clothes is pretty key to getting a good supply for your new and exciting wardrobe.

If you live in London, you'll find a wealth of charity shops to choose from. Oxfam at the end of Kensington High Street is especially good (particularly for vintage fans) and the Red Cross shop in Chelsea is guaranteed to turn up a designer label or two. Have a look at this list of the best of London's charity shops http://www.standard.co.uk/lifestyle/london-life/the-10-best-charity-shops-in-london-10300874.htm. Worth a treasure hunting trip, even if you don't live in London.

Once you've decided where to go, grab your list of ideal things to find, your bag of loose change, and your canvas recyclable bags for life, and get off and explore. Some charity shops don't open at 9am, so check opening times, which may be 9.30 or even 10am, and remember that some close early too, often 4pm or 4.30pm. Most charity shops don't open on Sundays either, so check that online before you head off.

Most of the people who work in charity shops are volunteers, and they are freely giving up their time to support their chosen charity. Talk to them; find out more about the charity, or why they love to do what they do. It's always a fascinating conversation. If you're after something specific it is well worth asking as it may just be at the back of the shop. All the staff I've met are so helpful they'll even look out for something for you if you just chat to them and ask. We recently ran a photo shoot of this seasons coming trends with clothes found from second hand sources; the ladies in my local Helen and Douglas House charity shop were a godsend and kept back lots of things for me to look at when I went in.

When I walk into a charity shop, I'm like my pointer Dessie. You can almost see me, sniffing the wind, tail up, knowing there's a rabbit or a squirrel hiding in the undergrowth (or rather a gorgeous treasure hiding in the jumble). When I walk in the door, I have to resist the temptation to look at everything and I immediately hone in on colours that I know are right for me. I go to these colours and have a look to see if they are the right size/styles for me. It's a quick scan, and can take as little as five minutes.

Don't browse. When you've got inside the shop, resist the temptation to browse around. If you browse, you'll end up spending hours and feel that your search is fruitless or not worth it, and you might quit. Later on, when you've got the bug and some time available, then yes, by all means look at knick knacks and books to your hearts content, but for now, repeat after me; I am a hunter, not a browser.

When you've seen something you like, you must check it. This is key – there are five checks you must always do – fit, label, fabric, wash and quality:
1. Fit: the only way to check the size and fit is to try it on. Pre-worn fabrics may well have shrunk or stretched, so ignore the size label and try it on to see if it is right for you. Things can also look so different on the hanger that I've often overlooked something, only to go back, try it on and love it (and the reverse is true!). I don't think you should buy any item of clothing, either from the charity shop or from the high street unless you've tried it

on first. This particularly applies to vintage. Many true vintage items may not have a sizing label at all, perhaps because it was originally made to measure. Try it on, and remember that a lot of vintage clothes were cut smaller than they are today, so you might need to shop for a larger size.

2. Check the label – always look out for a good quality label – and if you're not sure of the designer, look for where the item is made – places like Italy and France often denote a quality designer. On vintage pieces, you may only find the name of the dressmaker – these items are not designer pieces as we think of them, but no less are a sign of real skill and workmanship.

3. Check the fabric – I always avoid the manmade fabrics and look for quality fabric labels such as 100% wool, merino or silk.

4. Wash instructions – if it's dry clean only factor in an extra minimum of £10 in the sale price to get it dry cleaned....is it worth it?

5. Check the quality...many times I've brought home a charity shop bargain only to find a hole in the seam, or a small bleach mark. Before you leave the shop check over every inch of the garment you want to buy to make sure there are no holes, marks or damage.

By now, I can feel you're itching to get out there and start hunting for your new second hand treasures. Go on, give it a go. Pop to your local shop, or just have a peek on eBay. Get started and have some fun. If you're already a charity shop pro, you're probably reading this on the bus or the tube in between charity shops anyway. If so, open up your bag and show us what you've found so far, I'm desperate to see! But before you disappear into the sunset armed with a wallet of small change and a bag for life, I'm just going to give you a heads up to the next chapter, because it's an important one. It's about what to do with your treasures once you get them home. It's also about how to store them and care for them, and what to do when you stop loving them and are considering divorcing them. So, if you want a happy relationship with your clothes, read on dear friends!

CHAPTER 6: CARING FOR AND ADAPTING YOUR TREASURES

If you've spent time hunting for your perfect treasure, you're probably going to be a bit miffed if the first time it goes through the wash it comes out the size of a small 2 year old child's clothes – I know because that has happened to me. It was a lovely little Jigsaw cardigan, and despite trying to shoehorn my eight year old into it, I sadly had to resign myself to the sad idea that I had inadvertently ruined it, and the only things I'd be able to salvage from said cardigan were the buttons and a lesson learned. Cardigan went in the recycling bank, and I went back to treasure hunting. I've since made it my business to learn how to look after fabrics and treat them well. After all, they work hard for us, so looking after them is pretty important if we want to keep our clothes in good working order.

When I buy second hand and find something I love, I don't want it to wear out. I know the chances of finding an exact replacement are slim to say the least. I want my clothes to last, I want to be able to wear and wear them, and enjoy finding all the different ways of putting them together in an outfit. Did you know by the way, that the more of us that keep our clothes for longer, the bigger the positive environmental impact we have? Just by extending the active life of our clothes for 3 months can lead to a 5-10% reduction in carbon, water and waste footprints (www.wrap.org.uk). By buying something you love and looking after it, finding ways to wear it that keeps it current, you're not only feeling great and looking great, you're doing something pretty great for our planet. Hallelujah, everyone's a winner.

The first lesson I've learned from my disastrous cardigan shrinkage episode (and please forgive me, it was early days for me), is to read the darned label. Clothing manufacturers put in these handy labels to our clothes to tell us how best to wash them. Helpful if read before bunging it in the machine and hoping for the best. Sometimes, clothes don't have written instructions as to how they like to be handled, often there's a series of complicated symbols that look like something from the early Greek archeological discoveries, which need to be carefully deciphered. You can find a run down of what the symbols look like and mean at www.en.wikipedia.org/wiki/Laundry_symbol.

Yes, the experts among you will be telling me now that there are shortcuts. We've all put things in the machine that should be dry clean only and found they've come out fine. I do wonder if some brands put dry clean only on all their labels just to be on the safe side. If you are in any doubt though, err on the side of caution when it comes to laundering, because as we've said, replacements are hard to come by with your new second hand treasures.

When it comes to laundering we are very fortunate. No longer does it take a day and muscles the size of Giant Haystacks to work the mangle in order to wash our clothes. All those washboards and lumping tubs of soapy water might have been good for our muscles, but with modern washing machines, they can do all the hard work while we get on and do something else.

And I wonder if modern machines are almost too convenient. How many times do you wear something before it goes in the wash? Once? Twice? Wear it until it walks to the machine by itself? Most people I ask wash their clothes after every wear. Which actually isn't very good for your clothes. Sure, if they've a dirty mark on them or they've got a sweaty odour about them, wash away. But if you've worn it once and not got it dirty, just hanging it up to air before putting it back in the wardrobe or drawer is all that's needed. Washing less saves time, money, energy, water, and makes your clothes last longer.

When you do launder your clothes, choose a washing powder or liquid that you like the smell of and the same applies to your fabric conditioner. Often I can be seen in the supermarket aisles, sniffing the bottle tops to decide which to buy. There is nothing nicer than the smell of freshly laundered clothing, especially if it's been dried outside in the sunshine.

When it comes to ironing said clothes, I quite enjoy ironing, but I have friends who will do everything they can to avoid it. One friend of mine tells me that by very carefully folding her clothes as soon as they are dry, she's managed to avoid ironing for about the last 20 years. She does pick fabrics on that basis though – the 'are they likely to crease, in which case I'm not interested' school of purchasing, which I would personally find too limiting. Most clothes do benefit from a quick press, especially if you line dry them as I do. I draw the line at ironing underwear, PJ's, bedding, and just iron the things that look like they're begging me to get straight again. The kids cotton school shirts, my jeans, Mr L's cotton polo tops, all seem to relax as the iron goes over them. If a fabric feels a bit stiff when it comes off the line, or looks all creased and unhappy, it just needs a quick press with an iron. Check the label if you're ironing something for the first time as some clothes are not at all happy to be ironed. Many a time I've run my iron over a pair of trousers, only to find I've made them go all shiny and horrid. Delicate and some man made fabrics usually benefit from a damp tea towel positioned between them and the iron. If you're in doubt about ironing something, first try putting it on a hanger and then hold the iron a couple of inches away from it and press the steam setting. Some fabrics just relax with a gently steam rather than a full-on iron.

Sometimes however, only a dry clean will do the job. Dry cleaning is an expensive business. And a bit of a faff, because you've got to take your clothes there, and then go back and collect them a few days later. For things like wool coats, suits, ball gowns, etc, you'll need to get them dry cleaned. The other thing I'd recommend you get dry cleaned the first time you purchase it is vintage wear (unless the seller has helpfully dry cleaned it for you). If you buy something and put it straight in your wardrobe, you might inadvertently introduce the dreaded moth larvae into your home. Far better to be on the safe side and make sure they don't come into the house in the first place. As an alternative, you can now buy odourless mothballs so your clothes will smell lovely and not like you've been to Narnia and back in them. I read somewhere that popping your clothes in the freezer for a couple of days also works to kill moths, but I've never been brave enough to give that one a try.

Once you've got your head around cleaning and laundering your new treasures, you'll want to turn your attention to storing them. In my time as a stylist, I've seen inside lots of people's wardrobes. Some are beautifully organized, and some are nothing short of a glory hole, a mish-mash of clothes long since relegated to the 'never wear it' category, Christmas decorations, a dry goods store of excess loo rolls, and even once a dog bed!

In order to be able to wear and enjoy your new treasures, you're probably going to want to store them beautifully rather than tip them in a pile and play outfit roulette each morning (although that option does sound fun.) So, let me take you through, step by step, how I teach my clients to sort and organize their wardrobes so that they can store their clothes in a way that makes choosing what to wear a joyful skip rather than a blood curdling scream of a job.

The first thing I tell my clients is that they should be able to open their wardrobe doors and wear anything that they find within today, so we need to start with a mammoth reorganization. It's a good idea to buy some of those storage bags that you can fill up and suck the air out. Not only will they be a good space saver, but also by sucking out the air, your clothes won't be susceptible to moths. It might also be nice to get some decent hangers as well. Wooden hangers are ideal for tailored clothes, and I like the velvet-coated hangers for my tops and dresses. Avoid the wire ones if you can, and make sure you also have some skirt hangers (with clips) and some trouser hangers that you can fold your trousers over onto. Put the kettle on and take an afternoon to have the most therapeutic of sort-outs that will get you started off in the best possible way in your new clothes life.

Start by taking out anything from your wardrobe that doesn't belong there. If it's not clothes or accessories, then it shouldn't be there. Put the wrapping paper and anything else that might be lurking somewhere else! Now, start to pile up your clothes on the bed, put all the dresses in one pile, put the tops in another pile etc. Pull out any clothes from wherever else you keep them too. Check the loft, other wardrobes, the ironing pile and even the laundry basket – you'll want to see everything you own for this task.

Now, firstly think about the season you are in. You can do this sort out at any time of the year, but with my clients, we do it twice; spring and autumn. If you are in spring or mid summer, you can quite safely pack away all your thick winter jumpers, Christmas outfits and coats because you won't need them for a while. And, if you're doing this in January, pack away all your maxi dresses, bikinis, and summer tops. Don't sort the out of season stuff at this point, just pack it into your new storage bags, and put it out of the way, you'll have fun re-discovering it all at the start of the next season, and you can sort through it then, when you can focus your mind on the coming season and decide what you want to keep.

Now, everything on your bed should be of the current season. Now comes the hard part - try on everything you have left. Don't just look at the label and make a decision as to whether something fits you; you absolutely have to try it on. Sizes vary so much between brands that the label is almost meaningless. Especially if you've worn and washed something it could end up bigger or smaller than when you first bought it, so make sure you don't skip the hard part and try everything on.

If you have a long mirror in the house, put it somewhere near where you're working, as it's very useful to look at your clothes in a full-length mirror. If you don't have one, it's worth investing in one – hang one on the back of a wardrobe door if you're short on space – it's really important that you see the whole outfit. With everything you try on, ask yourself these questions:

Do these clothes fit me well?
Do I like it?
When was the last time I wore it?
Does it fit my new idea of my shape?
Does the colour suit me?
Does this item of clothing work in terms of the image I want to project?

If you like it, it suits you and it fits you, that's great. Now, can you make an outfit of it? What have you got that it goes with? Do you have a necklace, or a pair of shoes or boots? Get creative and see if you can make at least one outfit from the item you've started with. Does it all work together? If so, take a quick selfie photo either on your camera or your phone. Keep taking selfies of the outfits you like as you go along. When you have finished with that item, put it on a nice hanger and hang it in your wardrobe.

What sort of things should you be hanging back up in your wardrobe? Well, go back to the charts you made about your lifestyle in chapter 2 and think about hanging up the kind of clothes you're going to be wearing every day. If you've got a lot of evening wear, but only go out once or twice a month, perhaps you can put that in another wardrobe in the house? Or put it in a suit bag and hang it at the end of your wardrobe. You don't want to be rifling through ball dresses to find something to wear to meet a friend for coffee (unless your Maria Callas). If you're a jeans and t-shirt kind of girl, that's fine – hang up your jeans and t-shirts. If you work nine to five and chuck on a pair of jeans at the weekend, give your work wear the lion's share of the space because that's what you do most of. Put the jeans in a drawer if you're not wearing them daily. Your wardrobe should really reflect your lifestyle and what you do every day, but don't keep a pile for 'best'. If you like something and it's appropriate for where you're going, then wear it.

Personally, I hang my skirts, trousers, tops, jackets and dresses. I fold all my knitwear, jumpers, jeans, dog walk gear, camisole tops and t-shirts and put them in drawers. I find that works best for me, but you decide how you want to do it. I do find that knitwear seems to prefer being folded, on the hangers it's in danger of stretching out of shape at the shoulder.

When I hang things back in the wardrobe, I do it in order of type and then in order of colour. So all my skirts are together and are arranged in order from darkest to lightest. Then trousers etc. It makes finding the ideal thing to wear today so much easier, and it's easy to see if I've bought similar items without realizing it. I also like to have a bit of breathing space between the hangers, it stops the clothes getting all squashed and creased, but also means I can flick through in the mornings without the use of a crow bar. I learned a lot about organizing my clothes when I read the Marie Kondo book "The Life Changing Magic of Tidying". Marie recommends folding clothes in such a way that they stand up on their sides in the drawer. That way, when you open the drawer, you can instantly see everything you own, nothing is left forgotten at the bottom of the pile because there is no pile any more. Everything you own looks like a wonderful Benetton advert, beautifully folded and organized in colour order. It's revolutionized my clothes drawers!

It's hard sometimes to be objective, but if there's something that you haven't worn for some length of time, then ask yourself if you should continue to give that item space in your wardrobe now. You may even have items that you've never worn, or you just don't like anymore, or there may be things that don't reflect who you are now. Time to get rid. Go, on, pop it on the 'thank you but it's time to part ways now' pile.

Interestingly, we often have an emotional attachment to clothes. That dress you wore to your brother's wedding, or the jeans you were wearing when you met your husband – you might not want to let them go, not because you think you'll wear them again, but because they mean something to you or remind you of a happy or important event or person in your life. Think about keeping them in a memory box, or (if you're brave enough to do so) can you use the fabric in some way? I've heard lots of lovely stories of patchwork blankets sewn from bits of fabric from grandmothers' skirts. If you love something, you don't have to say goodbye to it, but just don't hang it back in your wardrobe. As you are sorting through each item, you want to be checking it for signs of wear, laundry and repair. If something needs repairing or altering in some way, put them to one side. We can tackle this pile later.

By now, you should (hopefully) have a few things hanging up in the wardrobe that you want to keep, you might have a few things that need repair, you may have a bag of out of season clothes, and you may have a couple of bags of clothes that are not the right size for you right now. On the floor should be a pile that you've decided are not right for you. This is the pile that needs to go; the once faithful workers who are being made redundant and need re-homing. When you have finished sorting through every item of clothing you own, then we need to sort out what you're clearing out.

If items are in excellent condition, or still have the tags on, you might want to sell them to recoup some of the money you paid for them in the first place. You can sell online on sites like eBay or Preloved, or you can find a local dress agency who might sell it for you, especially if it's designer wear or occasion wear. You might want to try a swishing party or give some things away to friends, or you may bundle things up for the charity shop.

You might have items on this pile that can be re-purposed in some way. Could you alter the length, adapt it, change it, dye it, or do something new and exciting with it?

If you have a pile that has really seen out their best days and you don't feel they would be suitable for anyone else to wear, pack them up and put them in a textile-recycling bank – every textile can be recycled. To find a bank near you, here's a handy link; www.recyclenow.com/what-to-do-with/clothing-textiles.

If you're done all the above and it hasn't taken you very long, then sit back and have a cup of tea and a slice of lemon drizzle and wait for everyone else to catch up. If you're still finding more clothes to heap on the bed, get a move on. If your bed has just collapsed under the weight of said clothes a) what were you thinking? And b) keep going. If you're drowning in clothes, you need to have a proper clear out and cut it down. A lot. I can promise you that we never need as many clothes as we think we do. There's a great project I talked about in chapter 2; project 333, which involves choosing 33 items of clothes that you wear for 3 months. It's the ultimate capsule wardrobe challenge so if you seriously want to challenge your idea of what's possible to live with (and live without) and be creative at the same time, check it out at http://bemorewithless.com/project-333/.

Now, what you have left in your wardrobe should be items that are ready for the current season, appropriate to you and your lifestyle, and they should all suit you and fit you! It will be much easier now to see where you might have some gaps - perhaps a cardigan or a pair of trousers in a great neutral colour will help to bring everything together, or maybe a skirt with a certain colour in it will mean you get more wear out of some tops. Sit down and make a shopping list of these items - this will help you to just focus on what you need when you are out at the shops! Also have a look at your buying patterns; are there similar items that you've bought over and over again? Being aware of these patterns can help you to break them, so you don't keep buying the same things.

You should now have a well-organized wardrobe, where everything inside fits you and suits you. Now, when you open the doors in the morning, everything you see you can wear now - choosing that perfect outfit each day should be easier and quicker! For a while you might want to pick out your outfits the night before, just until you get the hang of putting things together in your new colours and styles. What you can now do is create your own wardrobe catalogue. Use the selfies you've been taking of you in different outfits and print them off and stick them to the inside of your wardrobe door. In the morning when you don't feel like being creative or you're stuck for time, you can pick one of the selfies and re-assemble that outfit to wear. Also, when you first go through this process, you'll feel like you've got more gaps than clothes. A few scarves or necklaces will help change the look of a smaller wardrobe initially, and don't worry about it, this is a work in progress. For now, just keep wearing the things you like, and start to think about what else can go with these key pieces.

Remember how in an earlier chapter, we were looking at whether to create one wardrobe that is just for you, or to have different clothes for different roles in life? Well, you can adopt whichever strategy works best for you, but there is one category I don't want you to have in your wardrobe and that's something you're 'saving for best'. Today is your best day. I don't want you to keep anything for 'best'. I want you to wear it. If you've got something that you love that looks fab on you, don't save it for a special occasion, wear it. If you've got a top in your wardrobe that you absolutely love and looks great on you, think about how you can wear the same top across different roles in your life. Can you de-compartmentalize your wardrobe, so that you don't have categories such as 'work', 'home', 'going out' etc.? Sure, I know that there's a practical element to whatever you're going to be doing, but if you're buying a jacket that is the perfect style for you, you'll get much more wear, benefit and compliments if you can wear that jacket over a dress for work but also over jeans on a weekend. See what I mean? Have a look at your wardrobe, and see if you've been keeping different aspects of your life very separate, or if you can merge your core wardrobe by wearing things that are perfect for you across different roles and activities.

Lets now go back to that pile of clothes that you've decided need repair or alteration. If you've skills with a needle and thread, replacing a button or re-tacking a hem shouldn't be a problem for you, but if you've never had a go before, can you learn how to do basic repairs? Of course you can! Is there someone in your family who would be happy to show you? If no one can help, there's always YouTube or BBC videos that can show you everything from how to sew a button, to how to take up a pair of jeans. For more complex tailoring and alterations, if you don't feel brave enough to have a go yourself then a good tailor or dressmaker local to you should be able to help.

Now, what about the pile that need altering, or amending, or chopping up and using for other projects? Firstly, brilliant. The more we can re-purpose our fabrics, the better. If you have a pile of clothes that you're not wearing for whatever reason, remember that they become nothing more than rags to you, so your job is to either find it a new home or find a new way that you can enjoy wearing it. If you've got a dress you love but the length ends at an unflattering point between your calf and ankles, think how much more wear you'd get from having it cut to just below the knee. Darts are another big one – most clothes are cut for a set shape, and as we know we are all different shapes. If you're an hourglass, you'll probably always have trouble getting darts in the right place – don't be afraid to get a dress altered because you'll feel ten times more special in it knowing it fits you perfectly. And a well fitting outfit looks ten times better than something that has been badly cut or is ill fitting.

There are lots of wonderful ideas for repurposing and altering clothes on the brilliant website www.loveyourclothes.org.uk. Start by selecting one thing from your pile and just have a go with it. I keep clothes that I don't wear but perhaps love the print of, or have an idea for adapting. They go in a special box and every so often, my kids and I have a 'crafternoon' where we get out the box and make anything we like from the clothes inside. It's quite handy having girls, because I can cut things down and make something for them. We once made my daughter a dress from an old skirt and an old top of mine, which she absolutely loved wearing.

We're only a couple of generations away from women who made their own clothes, and probably wouldn't have owned very many, yet today, how many people make their own clothes versus people who buy on the high street? Programmes like the Great British Sewing Bee have helped a resurgence in the hobby craft of dressmaking and altering clothes. This skill seems to have diminished, but definitely not died out! In fact, making your own clothes seems to have become rather trendy once again. One of my clients regularly makes her own clothes (well, she is a creative spring person after all), and I always admire her creations. I know how much love and care she's put into its production, and I can see how it fits her perfectly, is totally unique, and a wonderful expression of her creative personality.

When my grandmother was young, she made a suit as her going away outfit for her honeymoon. I've got a lovely picture of her in it. She must have felt proud as punch to be wearing something she'd made. Do you think she would have looked after that suit? You bet! Would it have gone in the bin? Never! Like many of her generation, my grandmother would have looked after that suit for years, perhaps adapting it along the way to suit the changing fashions, but it would have served her well, and after? Well, she probably used the fabric to make something else. She was an expert at repairs, knew how to hand wash like a dervish (always on a Monday) and she didn't own a lot of clothes, but looked after what she had.

If you're a very creative person, you can have amazing fun with your wardrobe and a sewing machine. You'll be able to add in a trim here, or a new set of buttons there, even change a leg line or a skirt hem to create something that is completely unique to you. How marvelous is that? I love the idea that we can all be completely individual, simply by adapting and embellishing our wardrobes. If you are skilled on a machine, start a collection of fabric scraps, trims and buttons – experiment with dyeing some clothes that are the wrong colour, or even think about making something from scratch. It's a hobby that can quickly turn into a passion, so if you don't have the expertise to know where to get started, why not look into a local sewing class? Your local college should be a good place to start, you can learn everything about sewing and how to use a sewing machine, and who knows where it will take you; you might get into pattern cutting or designing your own clothes?

If you've got something that you feel is an unflattering shade on you, you could try dyeing it. I've had great success in the past in changing the colour of something so that I get more wear out of it. The Dylon kits you can buy at places like Robert Dyas are great, because you can do it all in your washing machine, and all you need is the kit, your items you want to dye and a couple of bags of table salt. You'll need to very carefully check your labels and any trim to make sure the fabric will take the dye; some man-made fabrics just don't dye. Dyeing works best on light coloured items that you want to dye darker, you won't be able to dye a dark coloured item lighter. White, cream, pale pink or pale blue, these sorts of things dye well and may mean that you get more wear out of something that you were thinking of throwing away.

Seasonal wardrobe changeovers stop you from getting bored with your clothes, and storing properly helps you to spot any gaps. Being creative means you can adapt and repurpose things to keep them current and interesting and unique in your wardrobe.

I've just closed my eyes to imagine your wardrobe. It has sort of fairy godmother glitter dust shining on the doors, and inside everything is beautifully arranged like an expensive boutique. Your wardrobe would make Sarah Jessica-Parker start to drool. Am I right? If you're not quite there yet, it's obviously a work in progress, but don't give up. Getting dressed should be a creative joy in your life, not a depressing panic. Make your wardrobe a place you want to visit, make it cool and funky or organized and practical. Give those Ikea adverts a run for their money and assign everything a home. After all, when you buy something from the shops, you're basically adopting it and offering it a home, aren't you? You don't want to neglect your charges, you want to love and care for them, wear them, take them out. By moving to a second hand wardrobe, I've learned to love my clothes again. I'm like Mother Theresa to my wardrobe. Well, maybe not quite on second thoughts, but I am good to my clothes. And along the way, I've learned that buying second hand brings all sorts of other interesting and exciting changes....

CHAPTER 7: WHAT YOU CAN EXPECT TO HAPPEN AFTER A YEAR

My year of saying no to new taught me many things. It was also in many ways a re-discovery of things I had loved when I was younger, that I had completely forgotten. It rekindled my passion for clothes and my enjoyment of my own wardrobe, and I was amazed and delighted with the incredible feedback I got from others about my challenge. I learned a lot along the way; like the fact that you can't avoid buying some things new, and that there's always more choice secondhand than we think there is. I also learned that we perhaps don't need as many clothes in our wardrobes as we think we do. During my year, no one took me to one side and told me I looked like Bett Lynch on a bad day. I've felt cool, confident, and happy in what I've been wearing.

I read somewhere that in a woman's lifetime, she will spend an average of £90,000 on clothes, shoes, accessories, make up and hair care. That might sound a lot, but imagine if you live to 90, that's £1,000 a year, which is just over £83 a month. That doesn't sound like a lot to me, especially when it includes hair cuts, colour, make-up, and accessories as well as clothes. Perhaps £90,000 is a bit conservative as an average. Anyway, we spend a lot. An awful lot.

And some of it is a total waste of money.

We've all done it, bought something, probably in the sale, and probably because it was a bargain. That something has hung in the wardrobe for months on end, never seeing the light of day, finally to be bagged up and taken to the charity shop, still with the labels on. We make mistakes all the time. But I know for a fact that once you understand your rules of colour shape and style, mistakes drastically reduce because you have a game plan.

As well as saving by not making mistakes, I've also saved money by buying second hand treasures. Lets say that the price of an average pair of women's trousers in an average high street shop is £40. In a charity shop, they might be £6 or £7. I've even bought things recently in a jumble sale for 10p – and it was a lovely M&S skirt that probably was about £50 new. In fact, I believe that you can dress head to toe from charity shops (excluding your underwear) for less than £25. And that's including shoes, a bag and a necklace or bracelet. How much would an outfit cost from your favourite high street shop? I reckon that by saying no to new and buying secondhand, I've saved something like £800 to £1,000 in the course of one year easily.

As well as financial savings, saying no to new has brought me huge changes in my style and confidence. When I get dressed now, I have some basic things in good quality and everything else in my wardrobe I've either had for ages, or bought second hand. All my second hand finds come with a story about where I was and who I was with when I found them. I think that instead of restricting my style and choice, dressing from secondhand shops has expanded it. I bought a £7.99 Chinese silk jacket from Dorothy House in Devizes on a shopping trip with my sister. This jacket is blue on one side and cream on the other and is reversible, unique, and utterly divine. I've tried it over vest tops and long sleeved silk shirts, it works brilliantly with my good jeans (Abercrombie's £7 from Scope), and I think makes the outfit. I love this jacket, I love where it came from, I love what I can put it with, and I love that it makes me think of my sister every time I put it on, and that I feel special in it. That was £7.99 very well spent because that jacket makes me feel confident.

I've got a few things like this jacket – things that make an outfit feel really me, and make me feel good. Even the dress I wore to my 40th birthday party is a Frank Usher bargain I picked up for £20. I think the fact I bought them second hand actually makes me feel even better about the clothes than if I had bought them new. New clothes often make me feel guilty at how much they cost. When I was buying new things, I'd bought a beautiful skirt in the sale from Jigsaw. Even though it was in the sale, it was still really expensive, dry clean only, and came all wrapped up in tissue paper. I loved this skirt and resolved to get my moneys worth by wearing it as much as possible. The first time I wore it, I snagged it on a rose bush and made an irreparable tear right across the front.

I felt so bad about that skirt.

Nowadays I think really hard before getting rid of any clothes. After all, they've been lovingly sourced and earned their place in my wardrobe because they fit my rules, and I might not find a replacement ever again. So, I task myself to find another way to use or wear it before ditching it completely. Can I dye it? Can I change the buttons? Can I just try wearing it with something else? Can I chop it up and make something new with it? I'm always trying to find new ways to wear things. I also find that creating your own collection of clothes forces you to be more creative. In high street stores, most of the work is done for us as the shop displays show you which top goes with which trousers and what bag to put with it. In second hand world, you're on your own, and the only rules to follow are your own colour shape and style rules. Beyond that, create away.

When I was much younger, I used to love charity shopping. My mum had given me an old Singer sewing machine, and I'd cut pictures of clothes I liked from the Littlewoods catalogue and then attempt to replicate them by chopping up and altering things I found in charity shops. I loved it. At university a friend and I started making our own ball dresses – usually on the day of the ball. Many a time we turned up in lovely unique handmade (and often quite lurid) dresses held together with safety pins, but I really enjoyed it. Back then the process of creating was fun and exciting and I wanted to see what I could make and adapt and put together. As I got older and started buying pale grey suits from Next for work, my wardrobe and my shopping habits just got very boring. All the fun and the sparkle went out of dressing.

I found I was wearing what everyone else was wearing.

Yes it was safe, but there was nothing new or different about the way I was presenting myself. And I began to hate shopping. I began to tell people that clothes don't matter, its what's on the inside that counts, but my inside was miserable because the outside just wasn't being what I wanted it to be.

Since re-discovering my love of charity shopping, my enjoyment of buying and wearing clothes has dramatically increased. I love watching the Great British Sewing Bee, and I've dusted down the sewing machine. I'm interested again. I want to play and have fun, and join in with it all. Much more exciting than that pale grey suit.

Another benefit is that I can now spot a bargain a mile away with one eye shut. I've definitely got the bug. Just say the words Jumble Sale to me and I spring up off the couch like a Labrador who hears the lead jangle. I'm ready. What am I looking for? Well, it's always something special. I only have to feel a bit of silk or whiff the suggestion of some real leather, and I'm hooked. I'm always looking for something that's unusual, different, or incredible quality (preferably all three). I don't want something that makes me stand out like Lady Gaga, I'm sticking to my rules of style, shape and colour, but I'm also looking for that something special.

The Treasure.

When I find something that I consider treasure, I do get very excited. Like the time I was in the Clothing Warehouse, and I found a pair of olive green mules. They had an unusual design on them, and I instantly saw that the label said 'Ferragamo'. I turned them over, and found to my delight that they were a size 6. By this point, I like them, I love the brand and they're my size – all pulse raisers in my world. Next I discover that they are genuine and ....wait for it...brand new. They still had the original sales label on the sole. Hyperventilating now. I try them on, they are faultless, perfect, incredible. The paramedic intervention came when I got to the till with these treasures – they were just £5.

Now that's hitting the mother lode.

Another good thing about this way of shopping is that I have a unique wardrobe. Let me explain.

The last time I bought a posh frock for a do from the high street was my sisters wedding 8 years ago. It was from Warehouse and was a Marilyn style cream halter neck with a full skirt and I wore it with a HUGE coffee and cream hat (because I was 'the sister') and coffee coloured shoes. I loved it. Up until the point, just as I was really enjoying myself getting in everyone's way with my huge hat I spotted a lady cowering in the corner – wearing exactly the same dress as me. If there was a soundtrack to this story, the music would get all dramatic right around now. She looked so sorry for herself that I just bowled over (two glasses of champagne and I think everyone bowls to some degree, don't they? Very difficult to glide effortlessly at the best of times and frankly far too much work.) So, I bowled over and said something like "Oh, hi! Haven't we got great taste?" with a big smile on my face meant to reassure her that it was cool. I think I must have frightened the living daylights out of the poor woman, because she looked at me like she wanted the floor to open up at that moment and swallow her whole, and me too for that matter. I laughed it all off, but I was genuinely gutted. Who wants to go to a lovely day in the same dress as someone else, especially when you're 'the sister'?

I don't think the other lady even stayed for the cake.

From that day on I was determined that this wasn't going to happen to me ever again, not if I could help it. And what I've discovered from saying no to new is that my wardrobe now feels really individual. I've got bits from here, there and everywhere – different brands, different countries, and different points in time, but it all hangs together because it works for me and my style. The last wedding I went to I wore a navy lace dress with a huge zip on it that cost me £4 and a lush floral duster coat that I bought on eBay for £35. I felt great and no one else would ever have had that combination of clothes, unless they'd also combined an eBay purchase with an 8-year-old pair of Roland Cartier's and had a trip to the Clothing Warehouse to find exactly my £4 lace dress. Unlikely.

When I first started talking to people about secondhand clothes, one lady said to me "Hmm, well I do go to charity shops from time to time, but I certainly wouldn't want anyone to know about it." And I wonder, why not? Is there a stigma to charity shopping anymore? If Helen Mirren can declare herself a thrift store fan, why can't we all? I started to wonder if everyone felt that way, perhaps it was just me who loved second hand, but in my time of saying no to new, I've met some really awesome people who share my passion. I love the way they dress, I love comparing treasures with them, and I love hearing about their latest adventures. These people have made their shopping and their image fun and enjoyable for themselves, and I always get very excited when I meet someone who says, "Oh, I picked this up in Cancer Research." I don't know about you, but I feel that it's OK now to say to people you love second hand shopping – blimey I've been doing it for ages and no ones scrubbed me off their Christmas card list because of it. I share my passion with people and I'm amazed how many positively respond. Just chatting to the Facebook group 'Say no to new' – they're a real bunch of cool dudes who love a rummage round the charity shops and often come back with real treasures too. And it's not a pastime exclusively for the ladies – I have several male clients, who absolutely love a bargain – show them a Vivienne Westwood t-shirt bargain on eBay or an incredible pair of Armani's and they're equally as happy as us girls.

Something that clients ask me all the time is how to stay 'current' or 'modern' while buying second hand. If you're a real lover of fashion, are you going to forgo that for the sake of buying from charity shops? Well you might not, but I hope our chapter on style has encouraged you to start your fashion journey with you and work your way outwards, rather than starting outwards and working your way in? Defining and developing your own style will always make sure you stay current, because the only person you have to be current with is you.

Having said all that I know for a fact that it is perfectly possible to dress to the latest trends and only shop second hand. During my year of saying no to new, I decided that we'd do a Vogue style photo shoot, but using clothes that were sourced second hand. We took 3 relevant fashion themes that were new at the time; 60's mod, fairytale, and folk and we sourced clothes that fit into those themes. Using the wonderful talents of Shannon Robinson and Anna Dora MUA, we created an amazing array of photos that really capture the looks. All the models are my own lovely clients who volunteered. If you want to see the pictures, you can have a look on my website – I especially love the fact that some of the outfits cost less than £20 for the whole thing!

So, there we are dear readers. I wish for you the same enjoyment that I've had from treasure hunting. I wish for you that amazing moment when you discover that the £4.99 top in your hand is actually designer, and fits you, and suits you, and is just divine. But most importantly I wish for you a feeling of confidence when you open your wardrobe doors in the morning. Confidence that you have clothes you love that say something great about who you are, so that when you show up for your day, your chin is held just that bit higher and your smile is just that bit bigger. Go get 'em, tiger, go get 'em.

LET'S KEEP IN TOUCH

If you've enjoyed reading this then I'd love for you to keep in touch. You can find me on Facebook on my In the Jumble page, or you can send a message via the website www.inthejumble.co.uk too. If you go to that site, you'll also find a photo album of pictures to accompany the book – I'd love for you to see the photo of my nan in that suit she made.

If you'd like to join others who are saying no to new, head over to Facebook and like the Say No to New page – we'd love to see you there.

If you'd like to find out more about services I offer as a stylist, you can go to my website, www.frankieandruby.co.uk. I've got some fab online courses you can sign up to if you need more help and advice regarding style, shape, colour, shopping, or organizing your wardrobe, or you might like to book a consultation. Either way, check it out, and do get in touch if you've got any questions, queries, or want to share your latest treasure finds with me.

I'd love to see what you've found.

Printed in Great Britain
by Amazon